WITCHCRAFT WORKS

VOL. 14

RYU MIZUNAGI

CONTENTS

CHAPTER 79 Takamiya vs. Alcina: Part 3

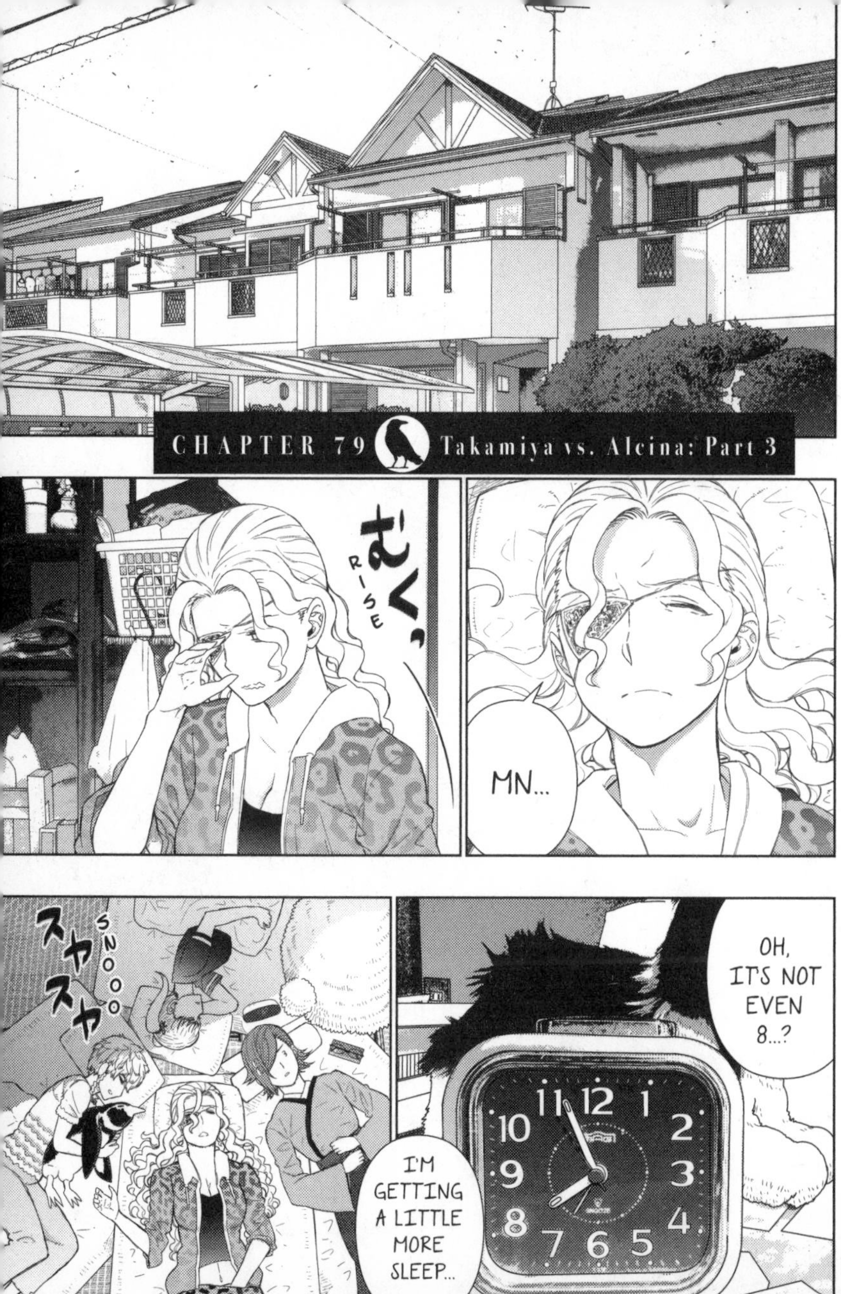
MN...
むく
RISE
OH, IT'S NOT EVEN 8...?
I'M GETTING A LITTLE MORE SLEEP...
スヤスヤ
SNOOO

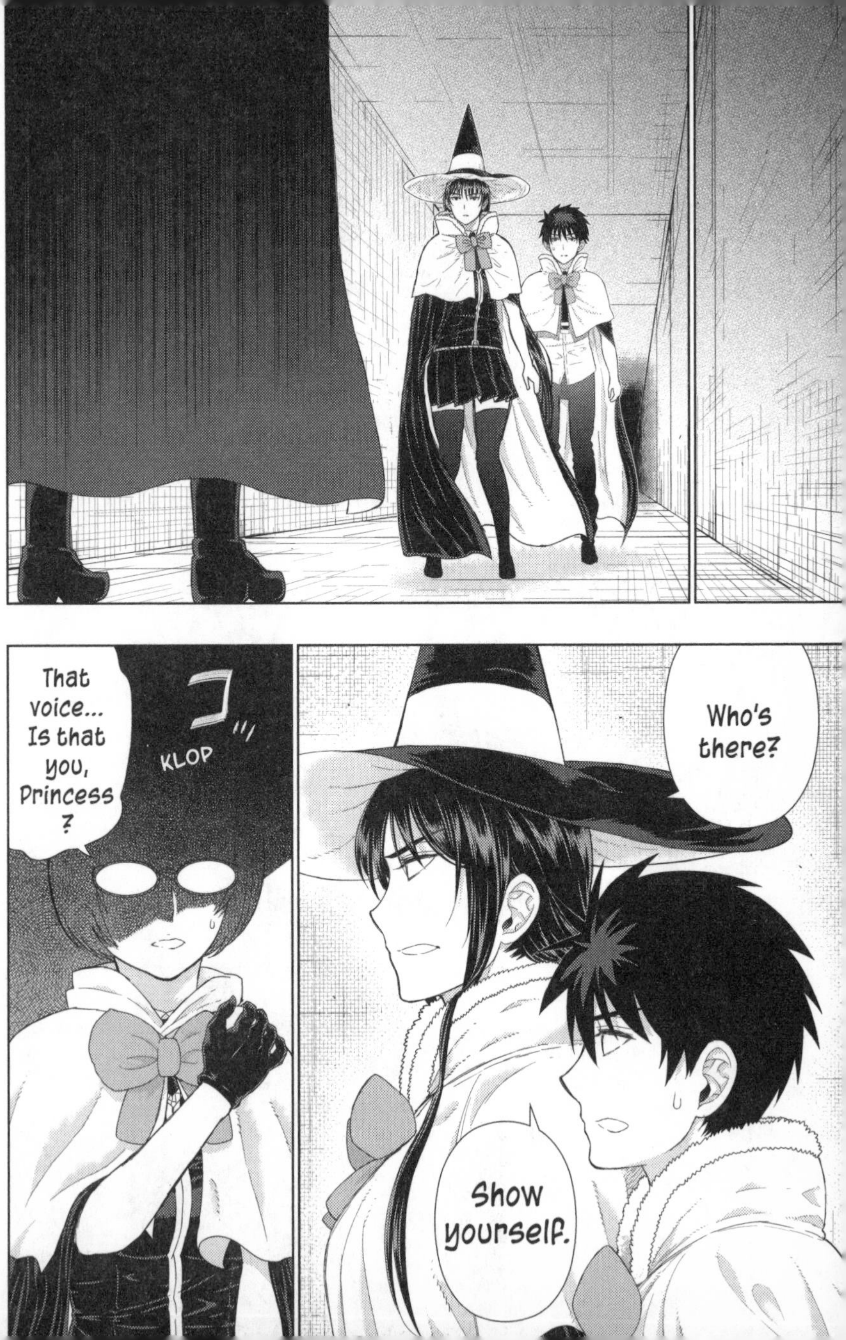
Who's there?
Show yourself.
ゴ
KLOP
That voice... Is that you, Princess?

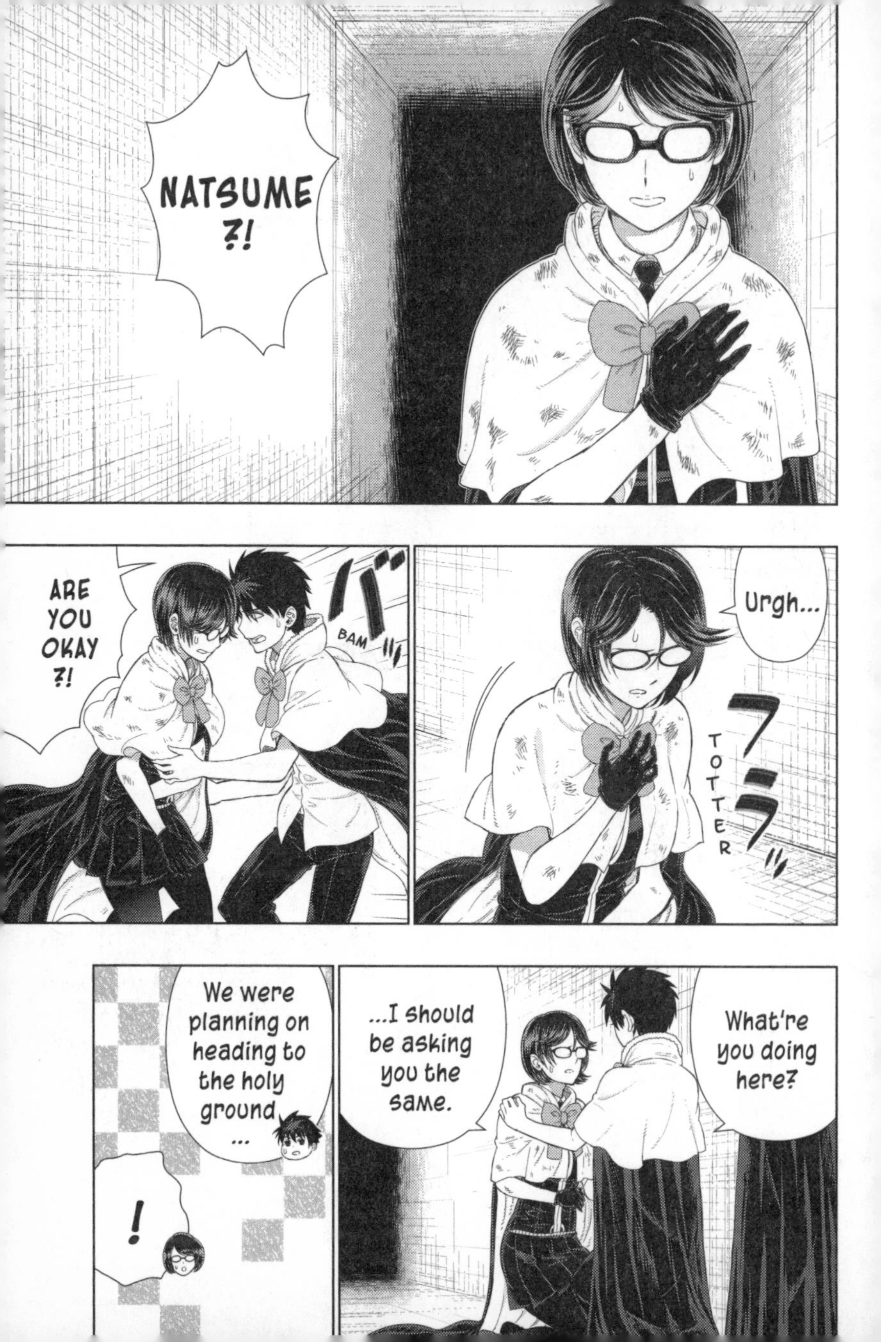
NATSUME ?!
Urgh...
TOTTER
ARE YOU OKAY ?!
BAM
What're you doing here?
...I should be asking you the same.
We were planning on heading to the holy ground ...
!

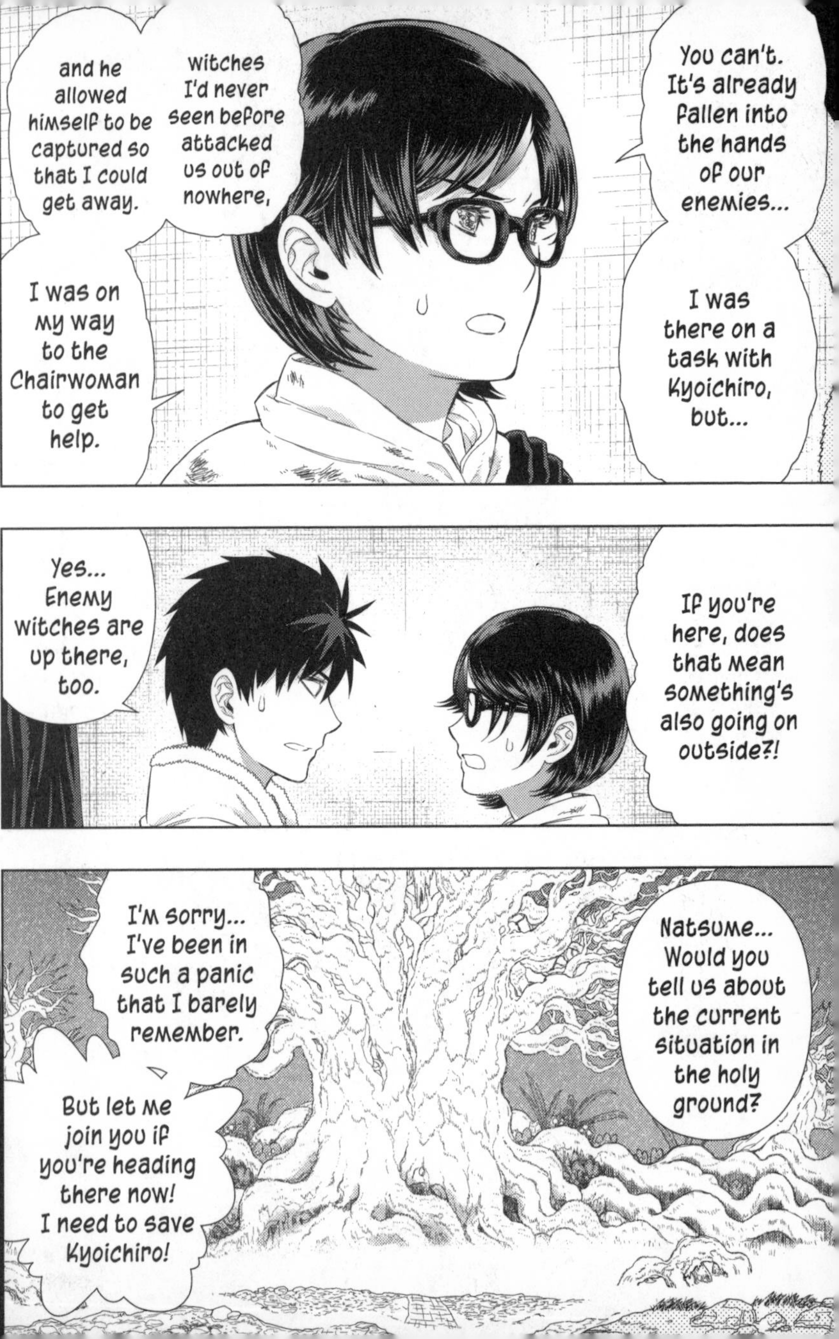
You can't. It's already fallen into the hands of our enemies...
I was there on a task with Kyoichiro, but...
witches I'd never seen before attacked us out of nowhere,
and he allowed himself to be captured so that I could get away.
I was on my way to the Chairwoman to get help.
If you're here, does that mean something's also going on outside?!
Yes... Enemy witches are up there, too.
Natsume... Would you tell us about the current situation in the holy ground?
I'm sorry... I've been in such a panic that I barely remember.
But let me join you if you're heading there now! I need to save Kyoichiro!

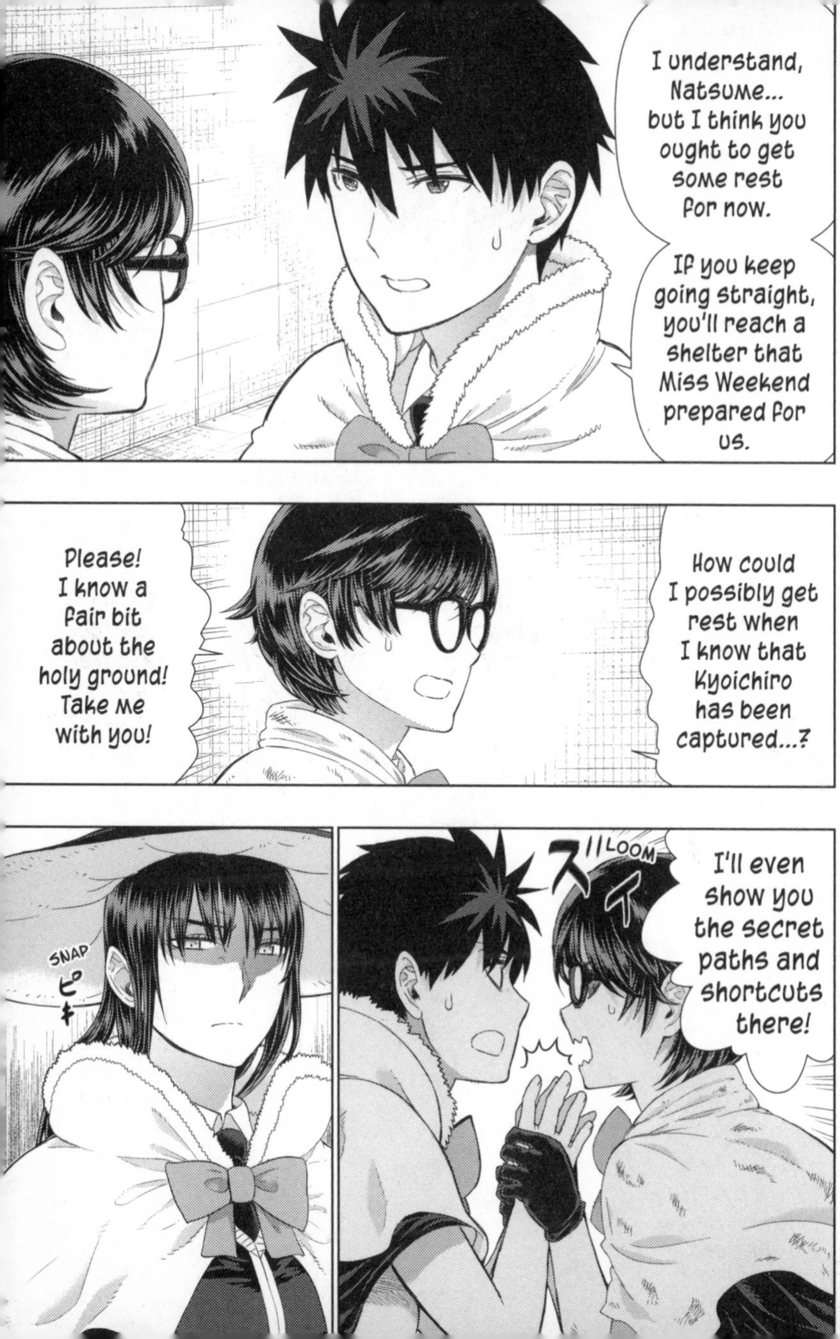
I understand, Natsume... but I think you ought to get some rest for now.
If you keep going straight, you'll reach a shelter that Miss Weekend prepared for us.
How could I possibly get rest when I know that Kyoichiro has been captured...?
Please! I know a fair bit about the holy ground! Take me with you!
スイ
LOOM
I'll even show you the secret paths and shortcuts there!
SNAP
ピキ

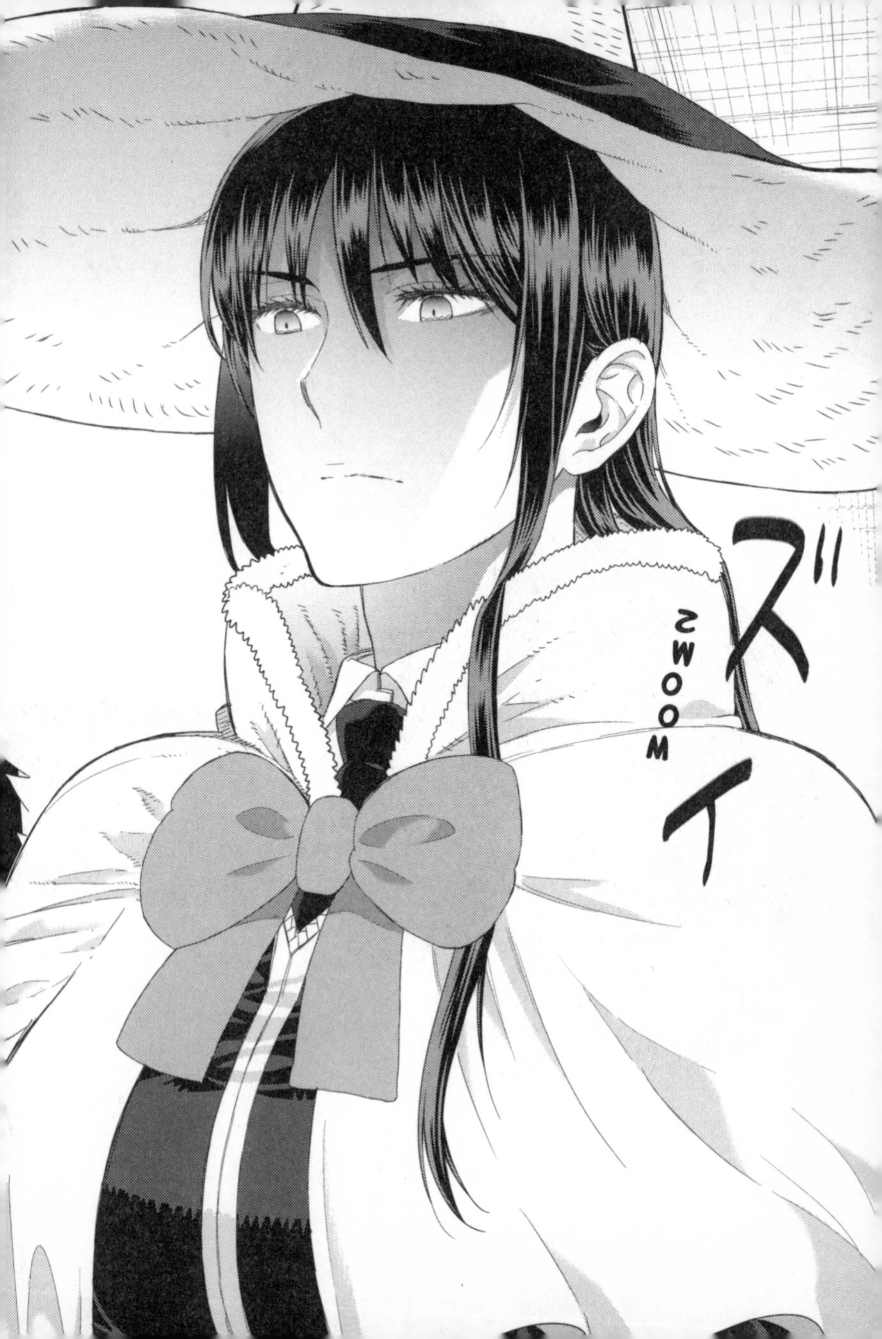
ズィ
ZWOOM

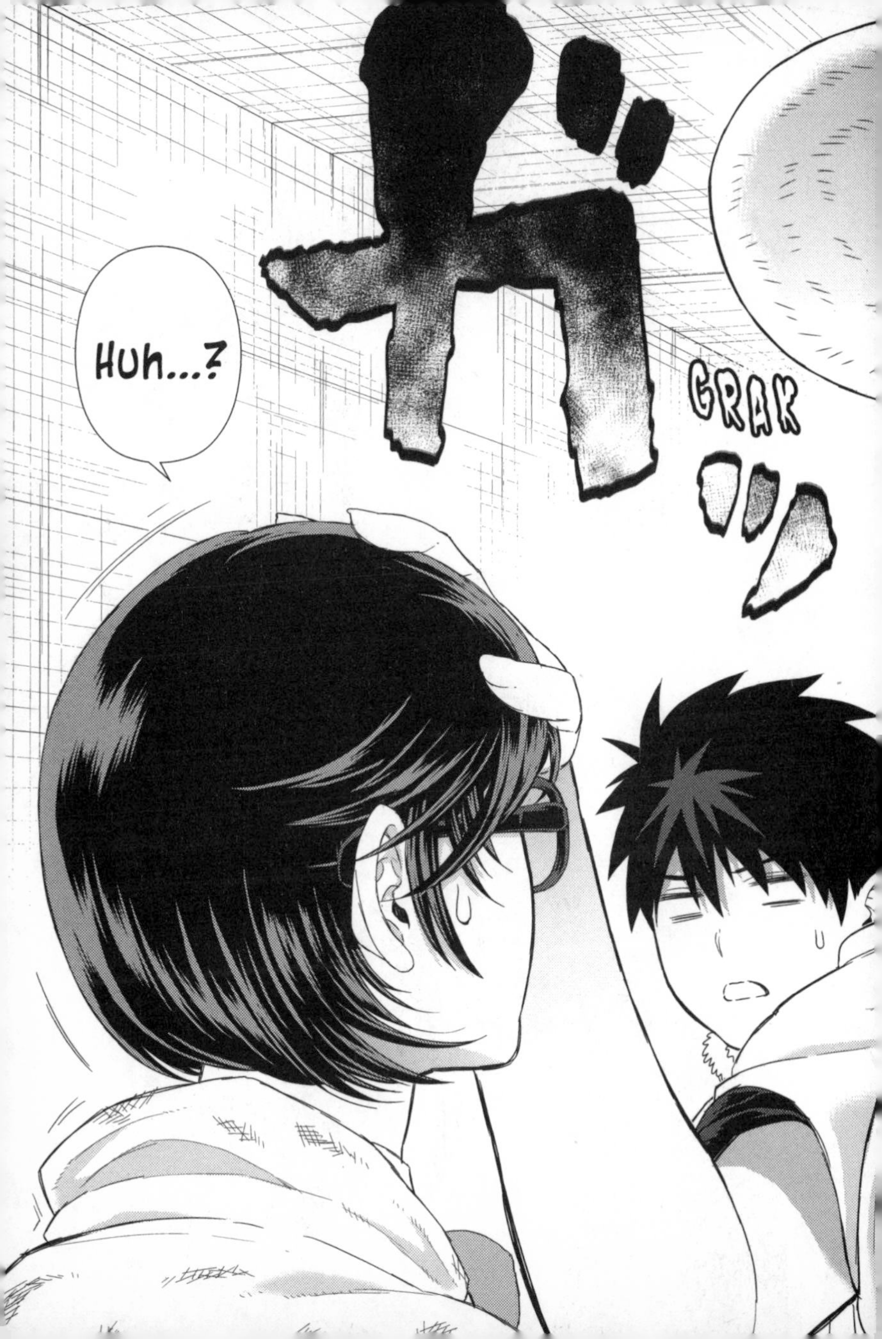
ガ
GRAK
HUH...?

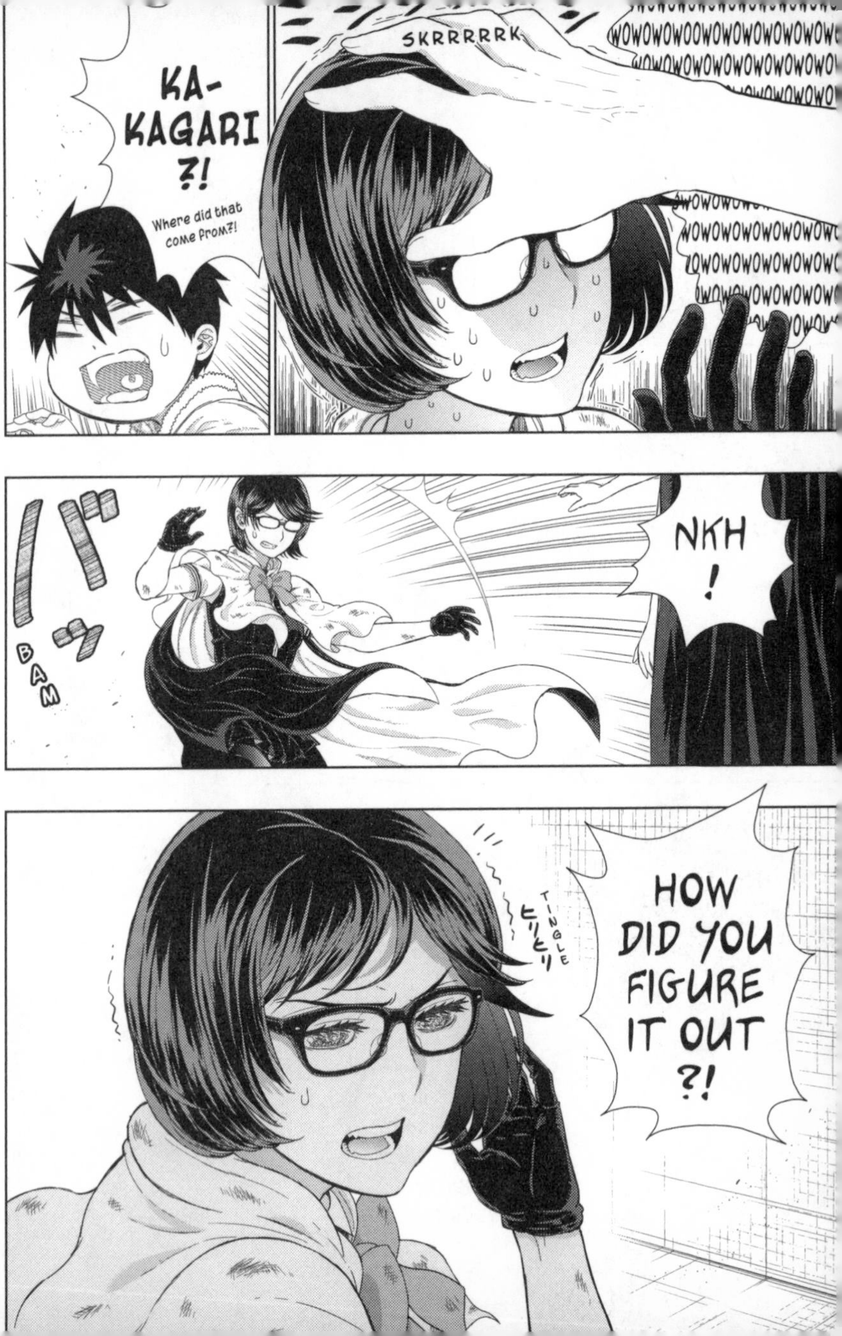
SKRRRRRK
KA-KAGARI?!
Where did that come from?!
NKH!
バッ
BAM
ヒリヒリ
TINGLE
HOW DID YOU FIGURE IT OUT?!

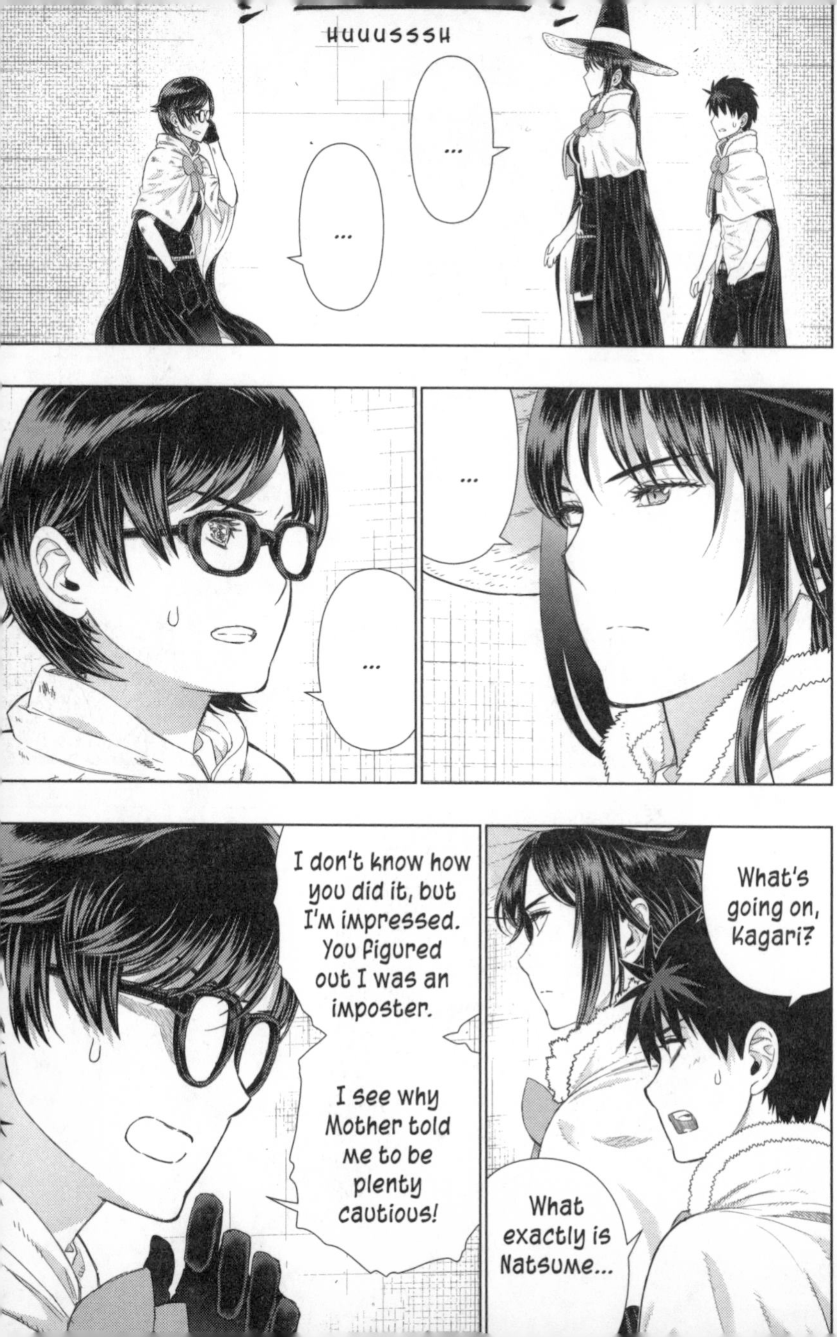
HUUUSSSH
...
...
...
...
What's going on, Kagari?
What exactly is Natsume...
I don't know how you did it, but I'm impressed. You figured out I was an imposter.
I see why Mother told me to be plenty cautious!

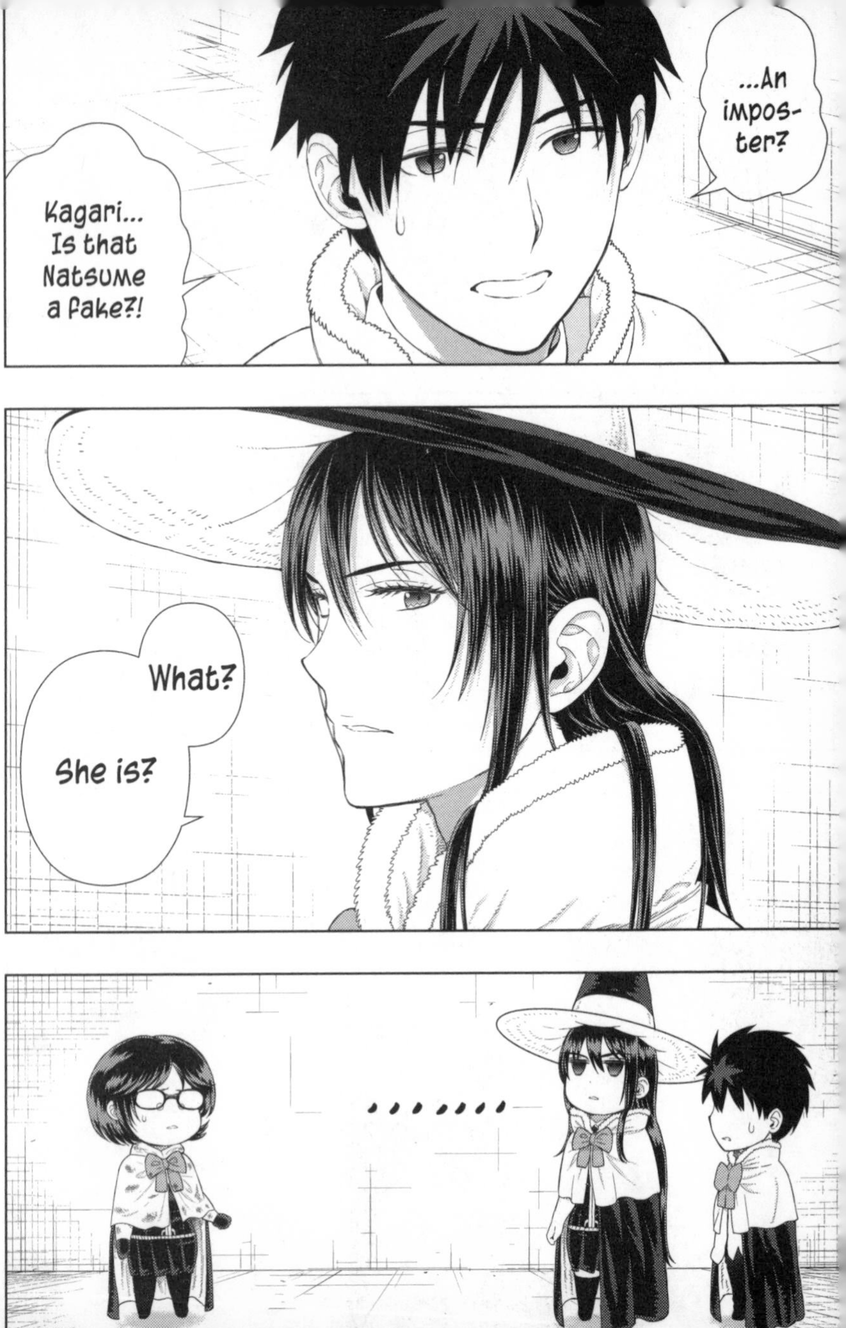
...An impos-ter?
Kagari... Is that Natsume a fake?!
What?
She is?
....

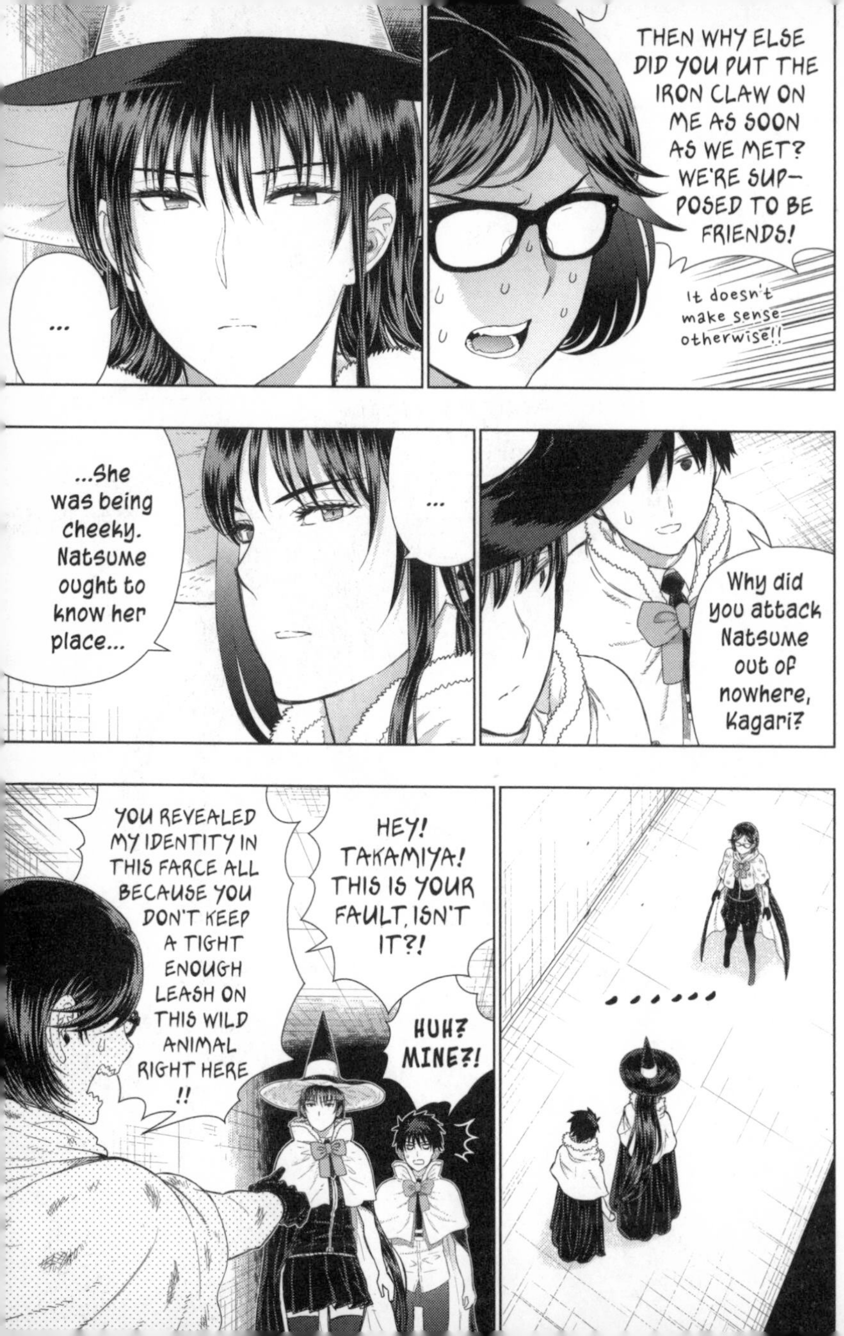
THEN WHY ELSE DID YOU PUT THE IRON CLAW ON ME AS SOON AS WE MET? WE'RE SUP-POSED TO BE FRIENDS!
It doesn't make sense otherwise!!
...
Why did you attack Natsume out of nowhere, Kagari?
...
...She was being cheeky. Natsume ought to know her place...
......
HEY! TAKAMIYA! THIS IS YOUR FAULT, ISN'T IT?!
YOU REVEALED MY IDENTITY IN THIS FARCE ALL BECAUSE YOU DON'T KEEP A TIGHT ENOUGH LEASH ON THIS WILD ANIMAL RIGHT HERE!!
HUH? MINE?!

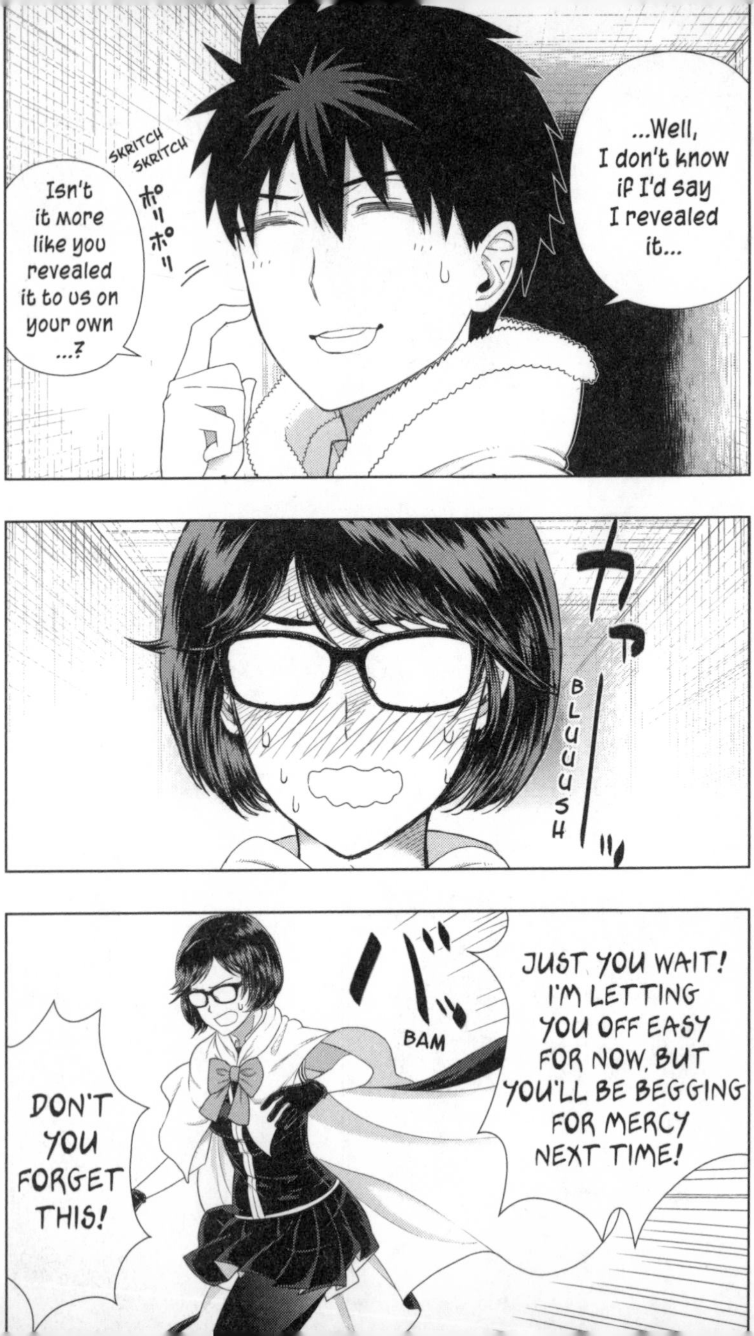
...Well, I don't know if I'd say I revealed it...
SKRITCH SKRITCH
ポリポリ
Isn't it more like you revealed it to us on your own ...?
カァ
BLUUUSH
バッ
BAM
JUST YOU WAIT! I'M LETTING YOU OFF EASY FOR NOW, BUT YOU'LL BE BEGGING FOR MERCY NEXT TIME!
DON'T YOU FORGET THIS!

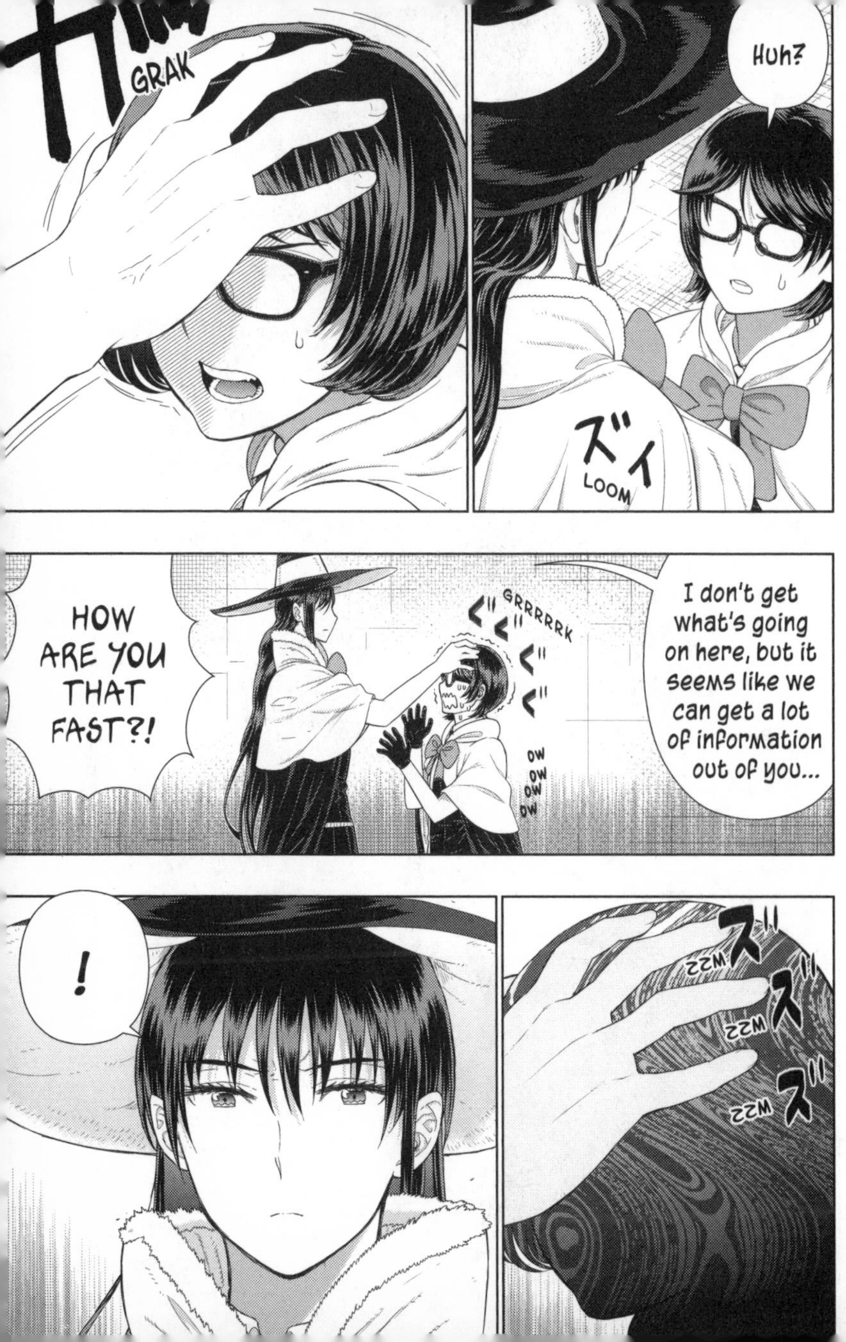

Huh?
ズイ
LOOM
GRAK
I don't get what's going on here, but it seems like we can get a lot of information out of you...
HOW ARE YOU THAT FAST?!
GRRRRRK
OW
OW
OW
OW
ZZM
ZZM
ZZM
!

That hurts, Kagari.

Kagari? If you're looking for me, I'm right here.

A-Are you okay, Takamiya?! ...I'm sorry. I...Why was I...

!!

AH

16

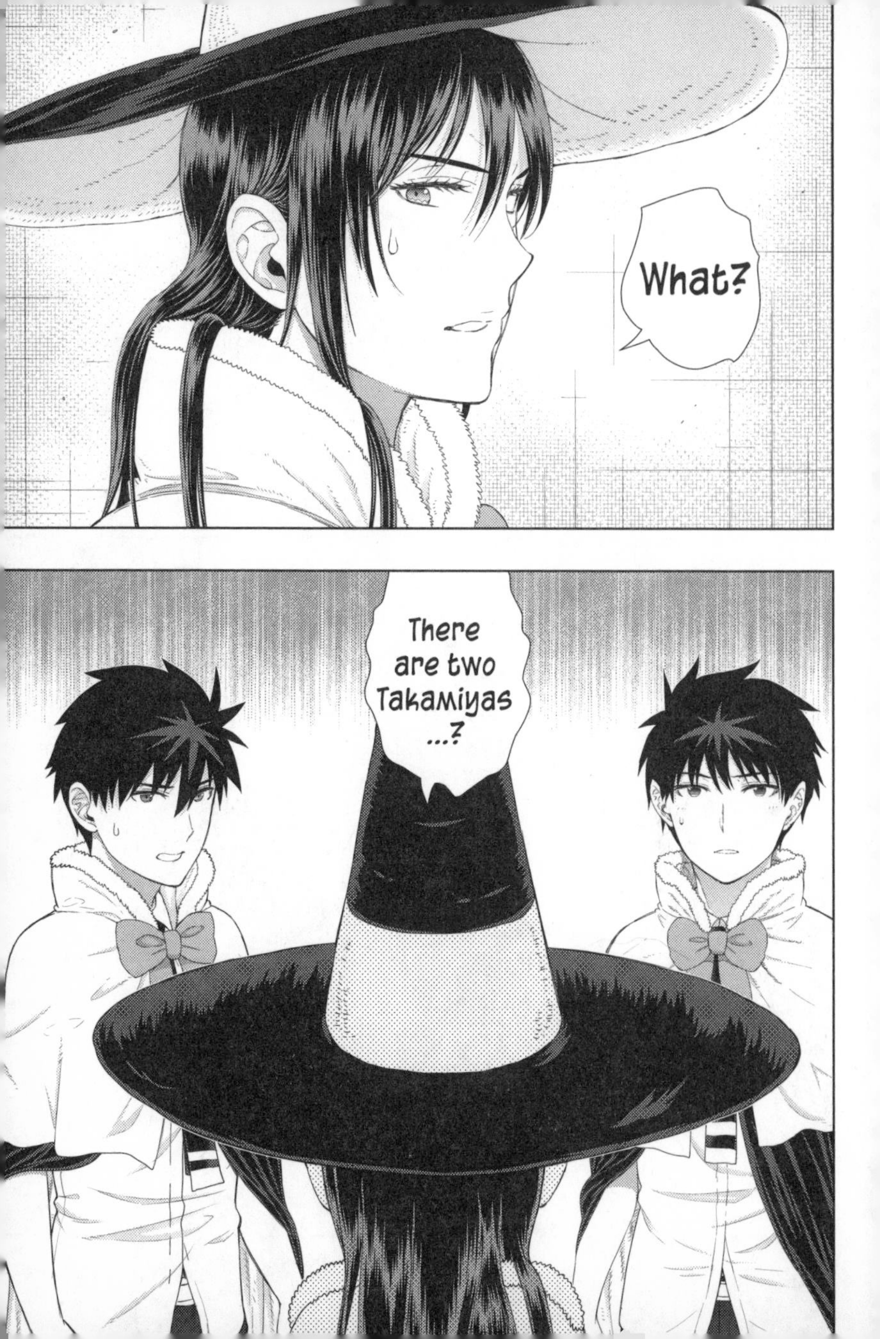
What?
There are two Takamiyas ...?

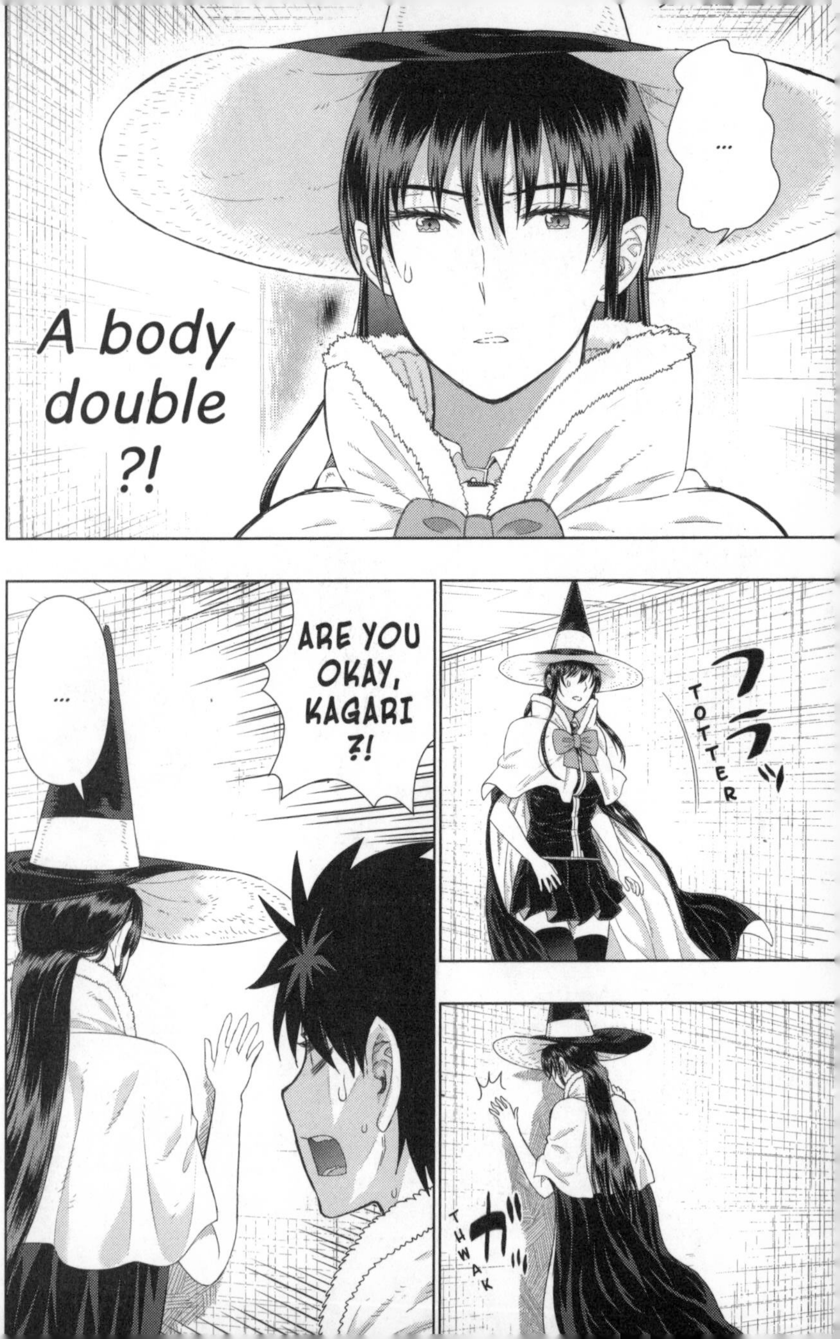
...
A body double ?!
フラッ
TOTTER
ガッ
THWAK
ARE YOU OKAY, KAGARI ?!
...

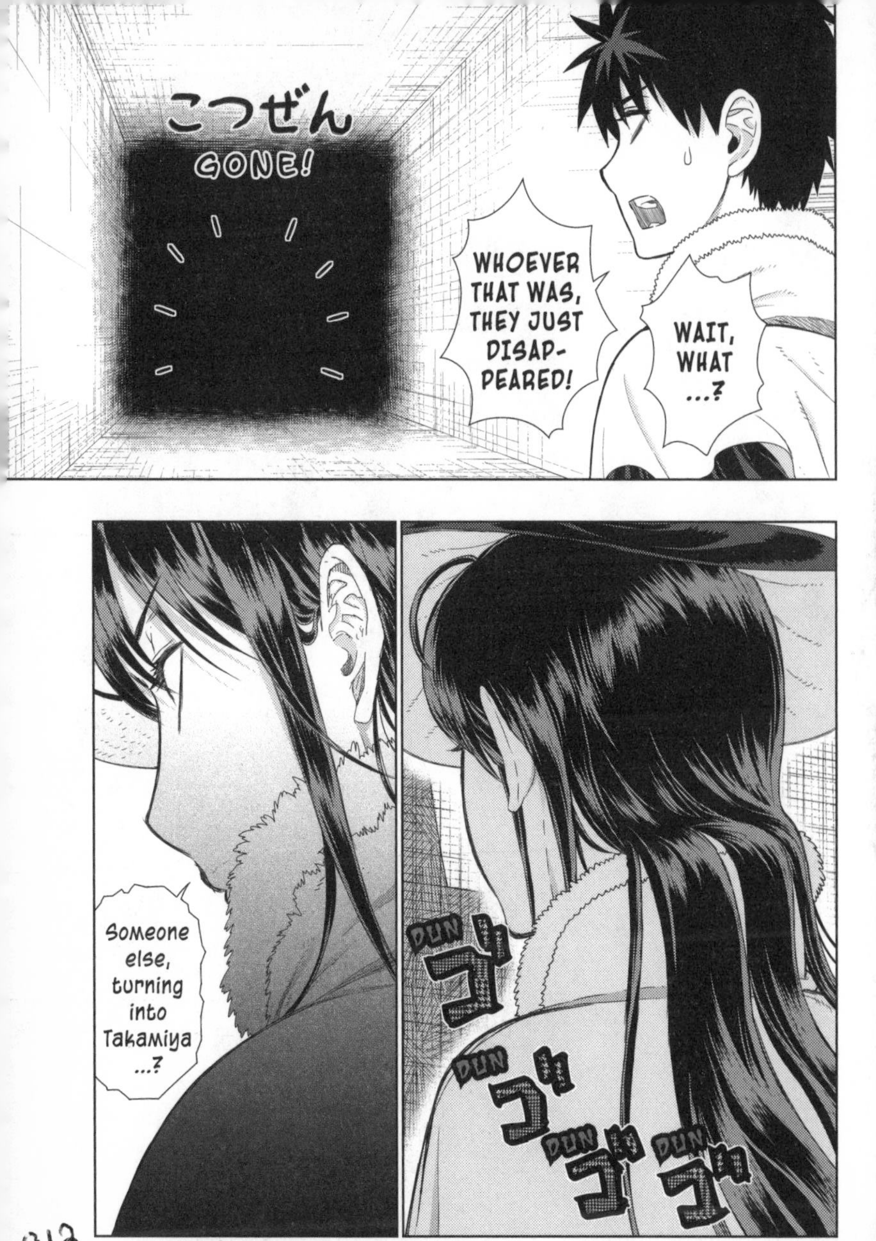
WHOEVER THAT WAS, THEY JUST DISAP-PEARED!
WAIT, WHAT ...?
こつぜん
GONE!
ゴ DUN ゴ DUN ゴ DUN ゴ DUN
Someone else, turning into Takamiya ...?

912

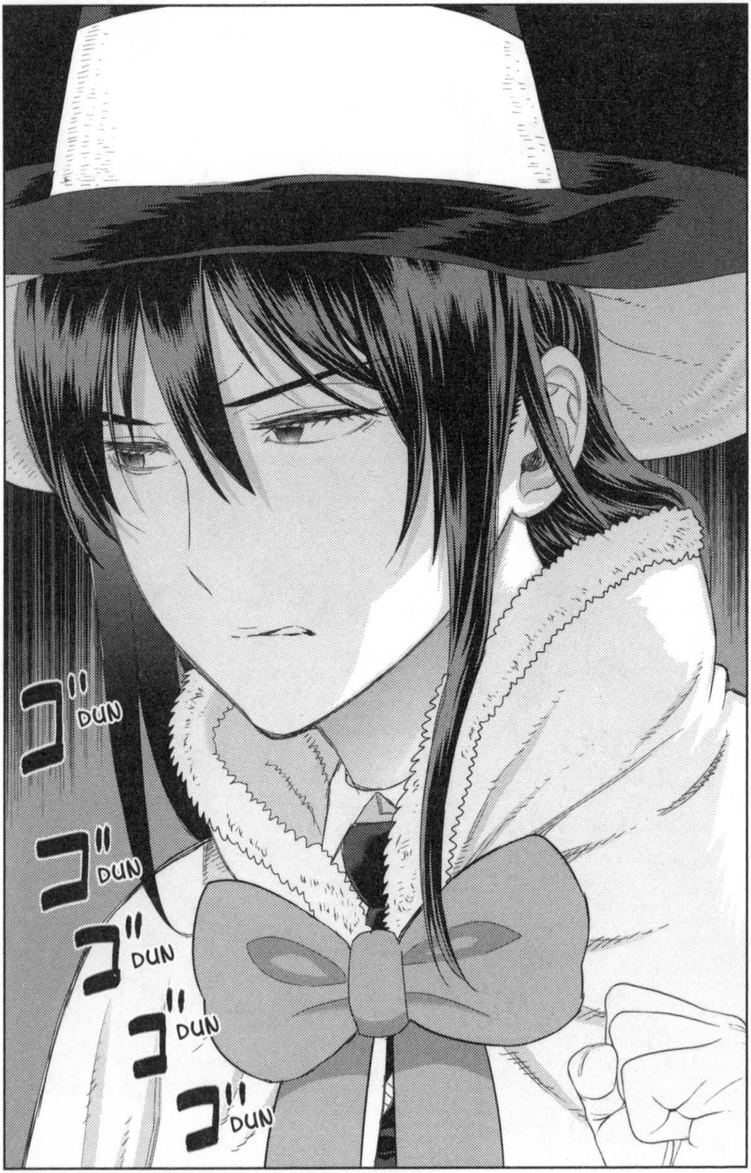
ゴ DUN
ゴ DUN
ゴ DUN
ゴ DUN
ゴ DUN

CHAPTER 79: *END*

Witchcraft Works

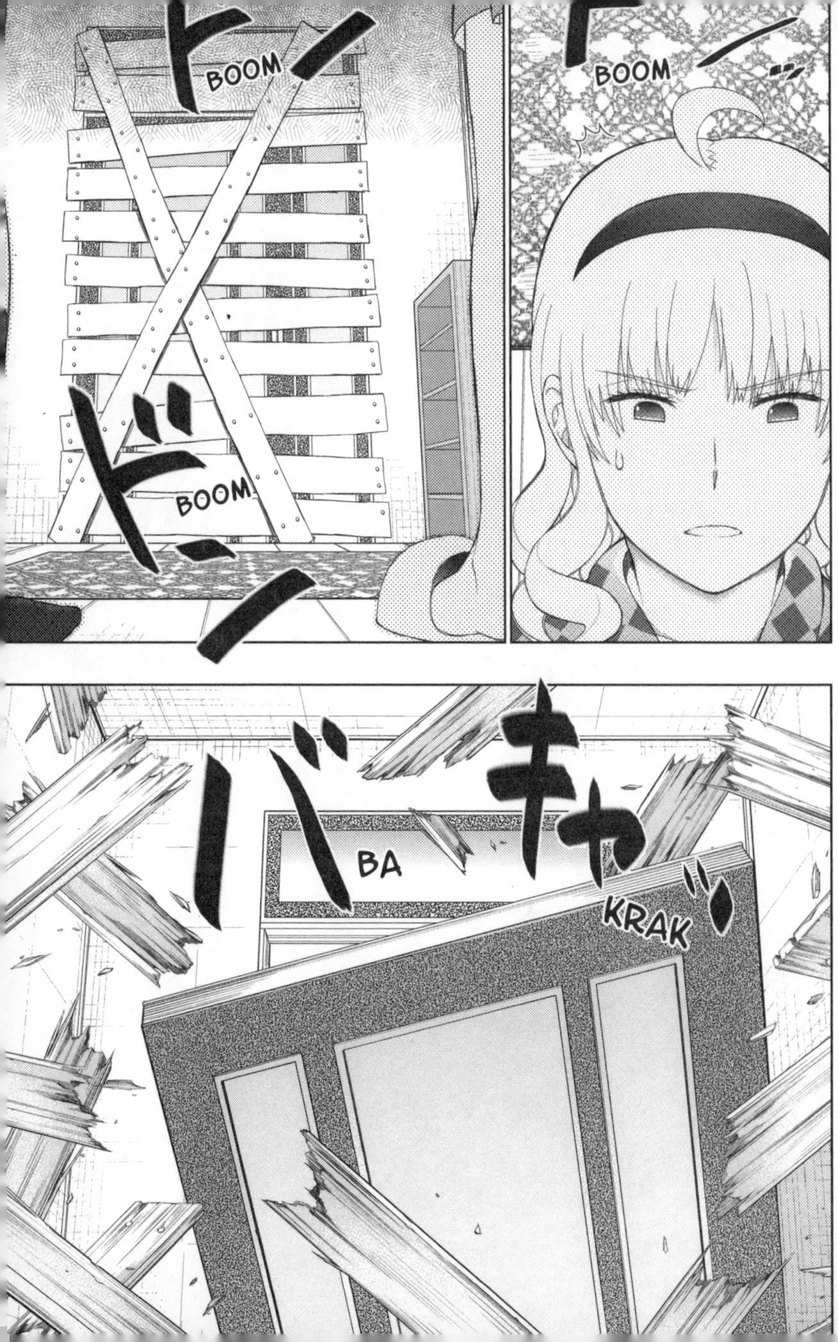
BOOM
BOOM
BOOM
バキャッ
BA
KRAK

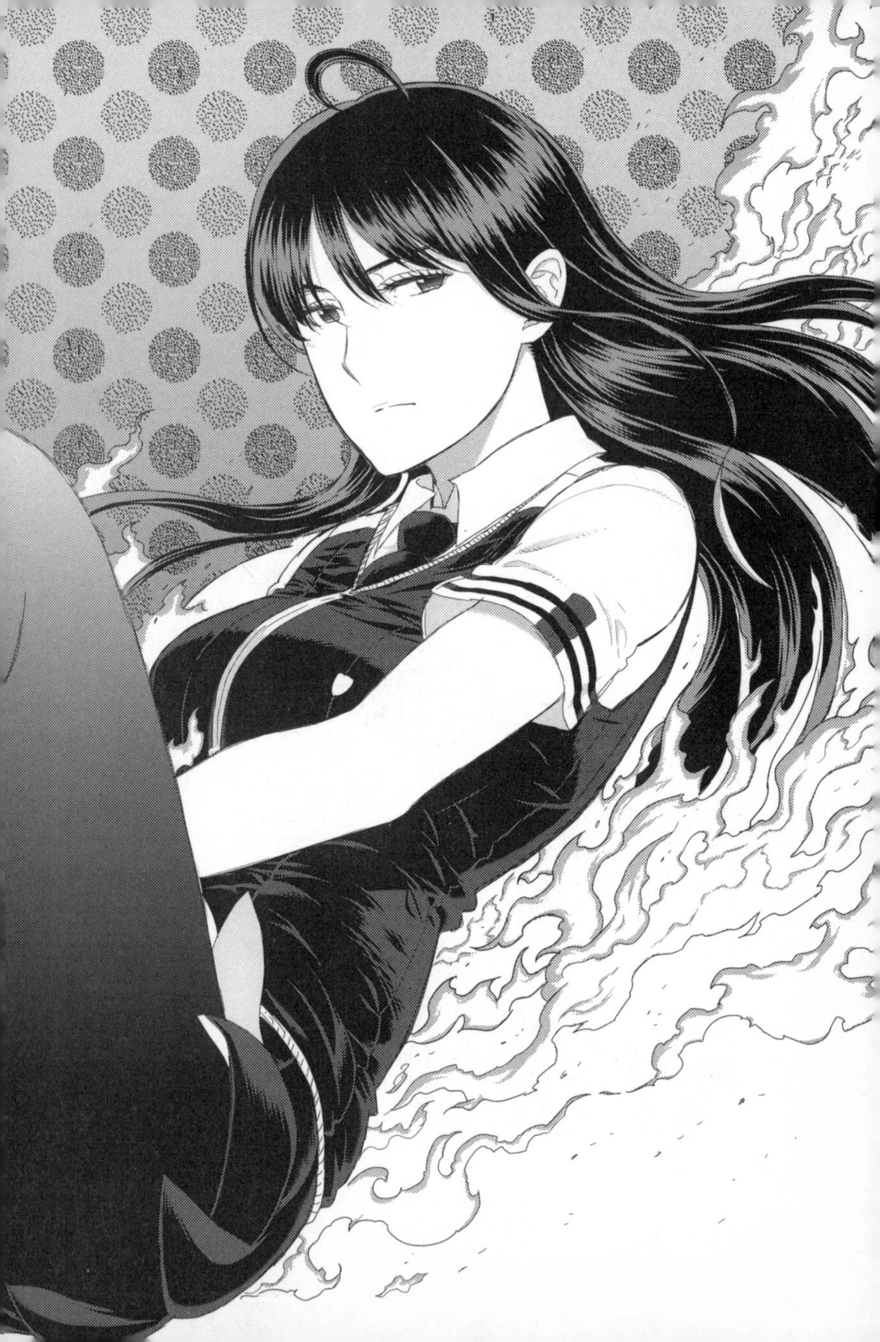

CHAPTER 80 Takamiya vs. Alcina: Part 4

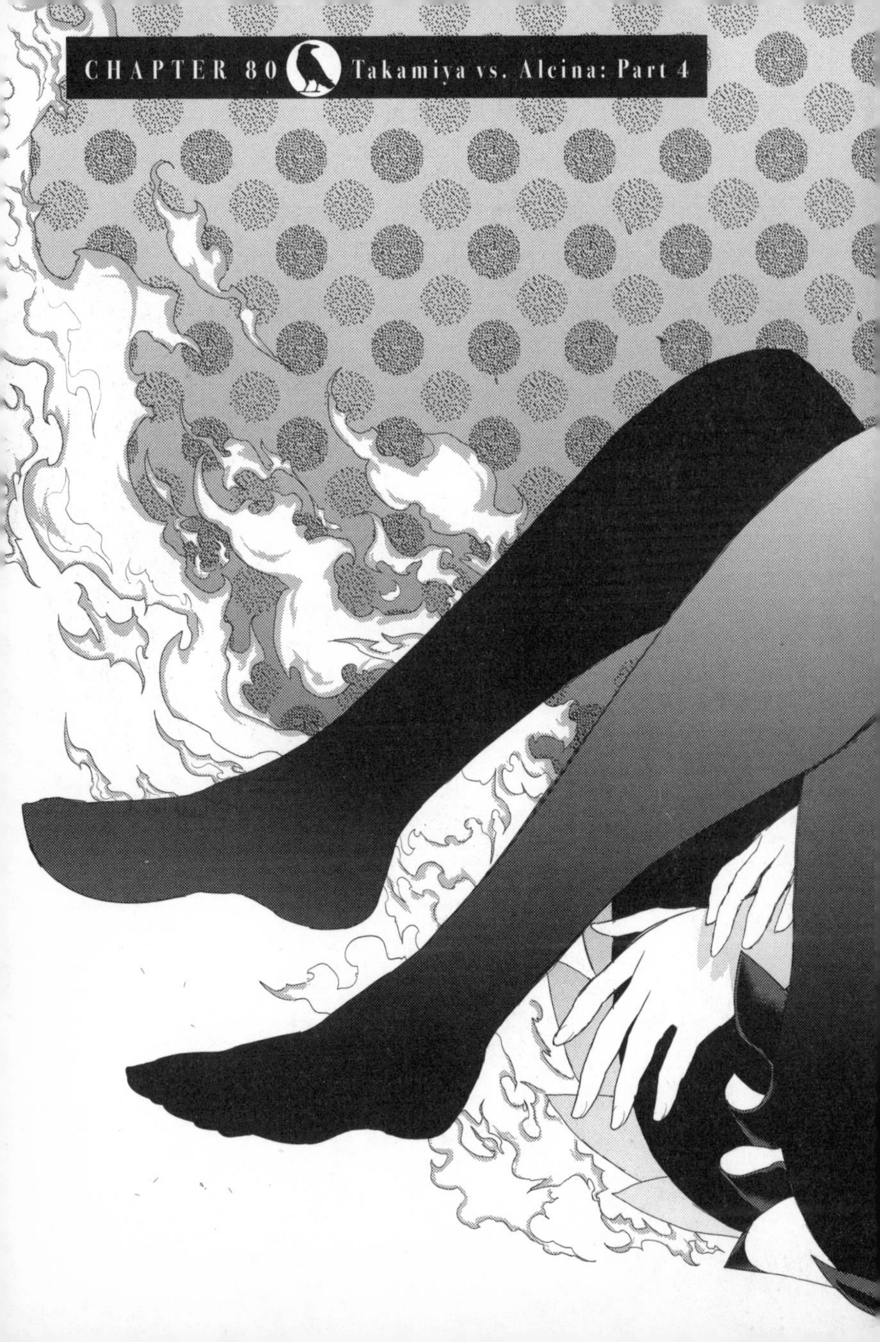

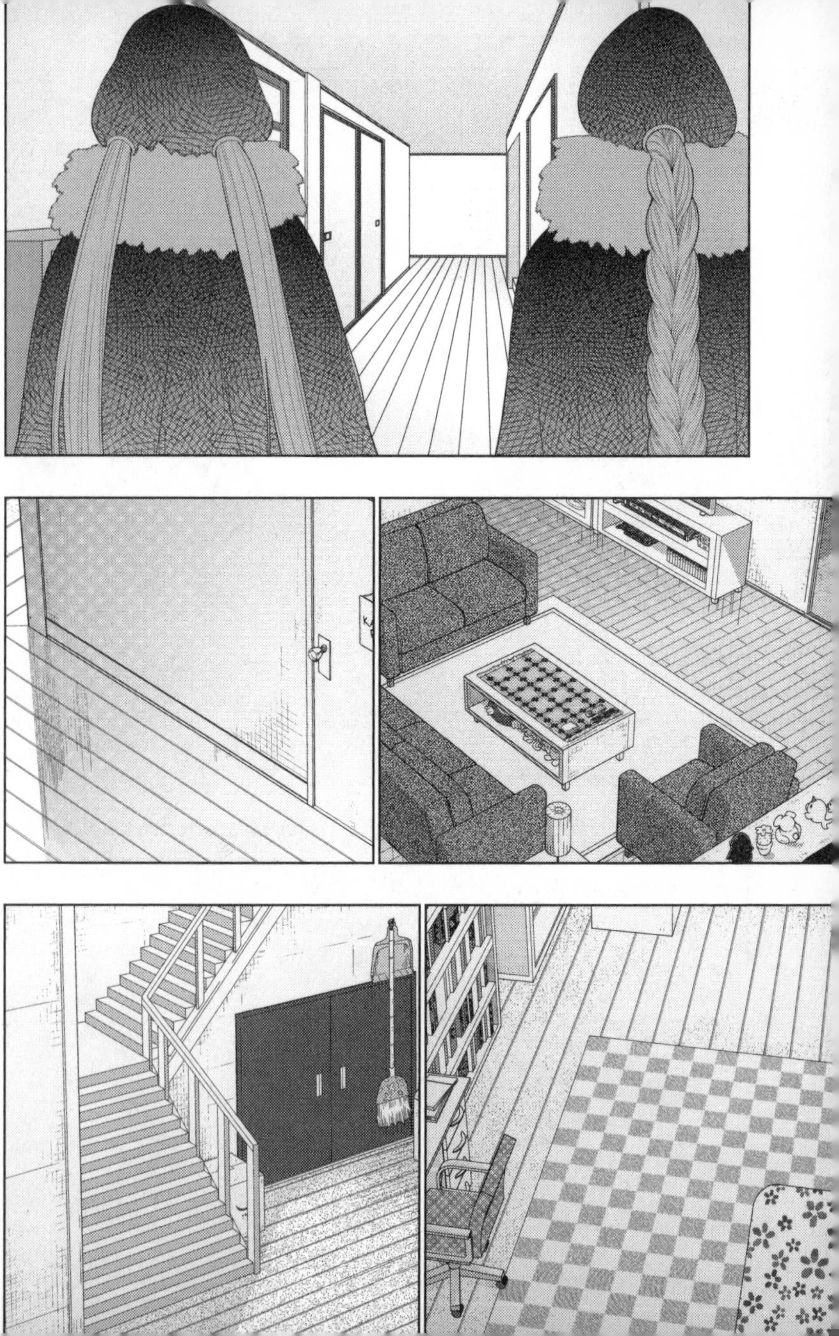

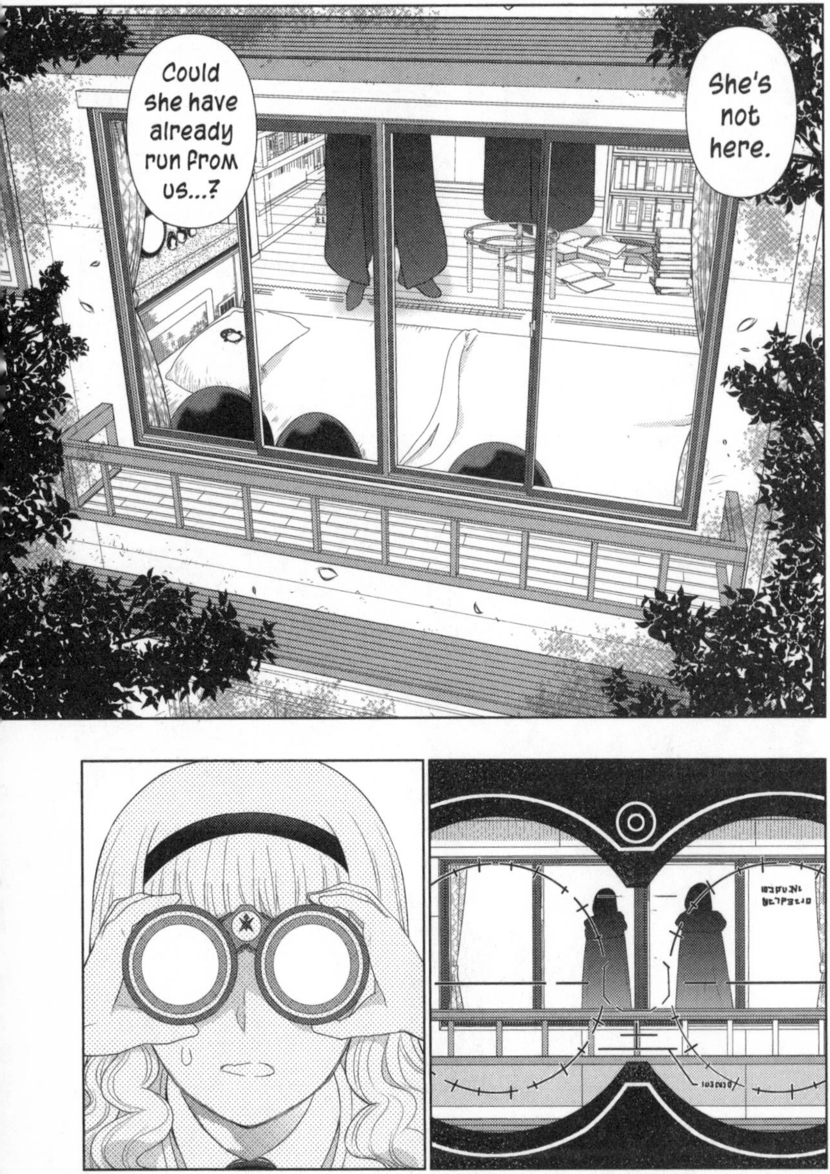
She's not here.
Could she have already run from us...?

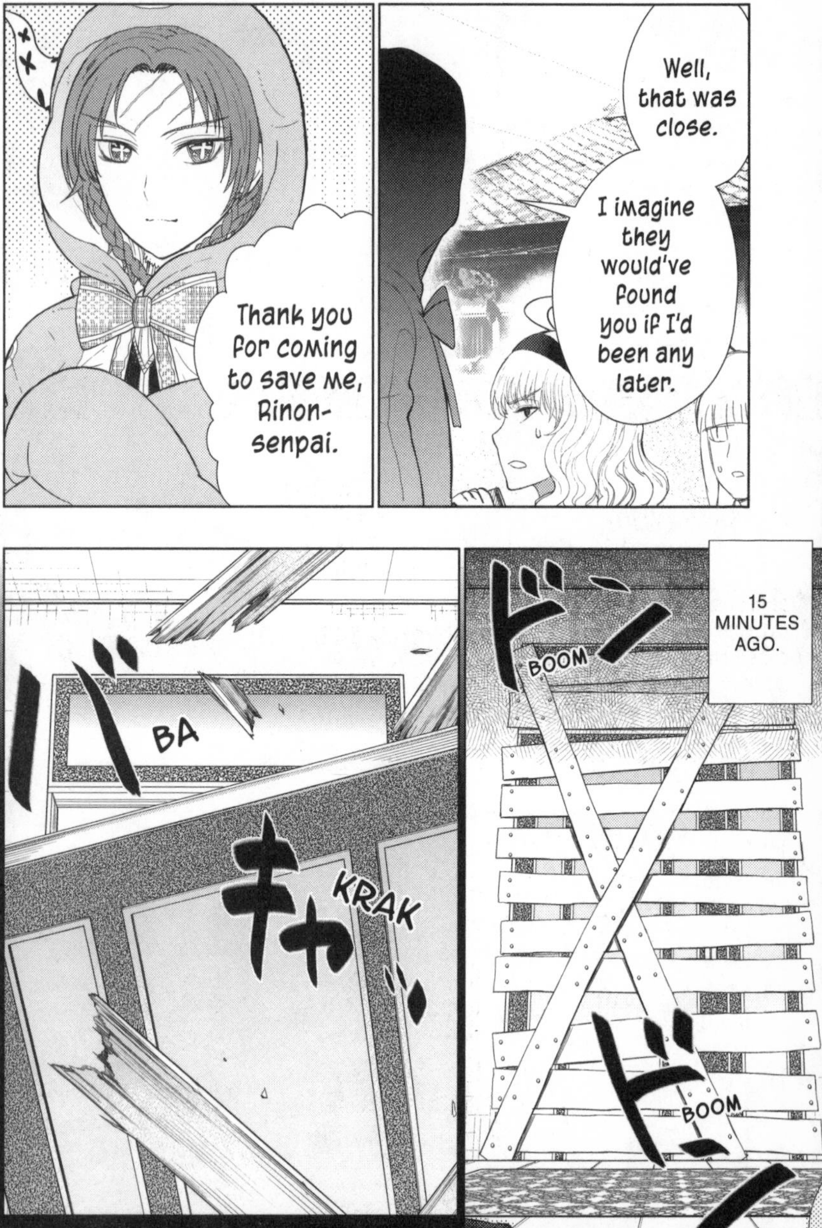
Well, that was close.
I imagine they would've found you if I'd been any later.
Thank you for coming to save me, Rinon-senpai.
15 MINUTES AGO.
BOOM
BOOM
BA
KRAK

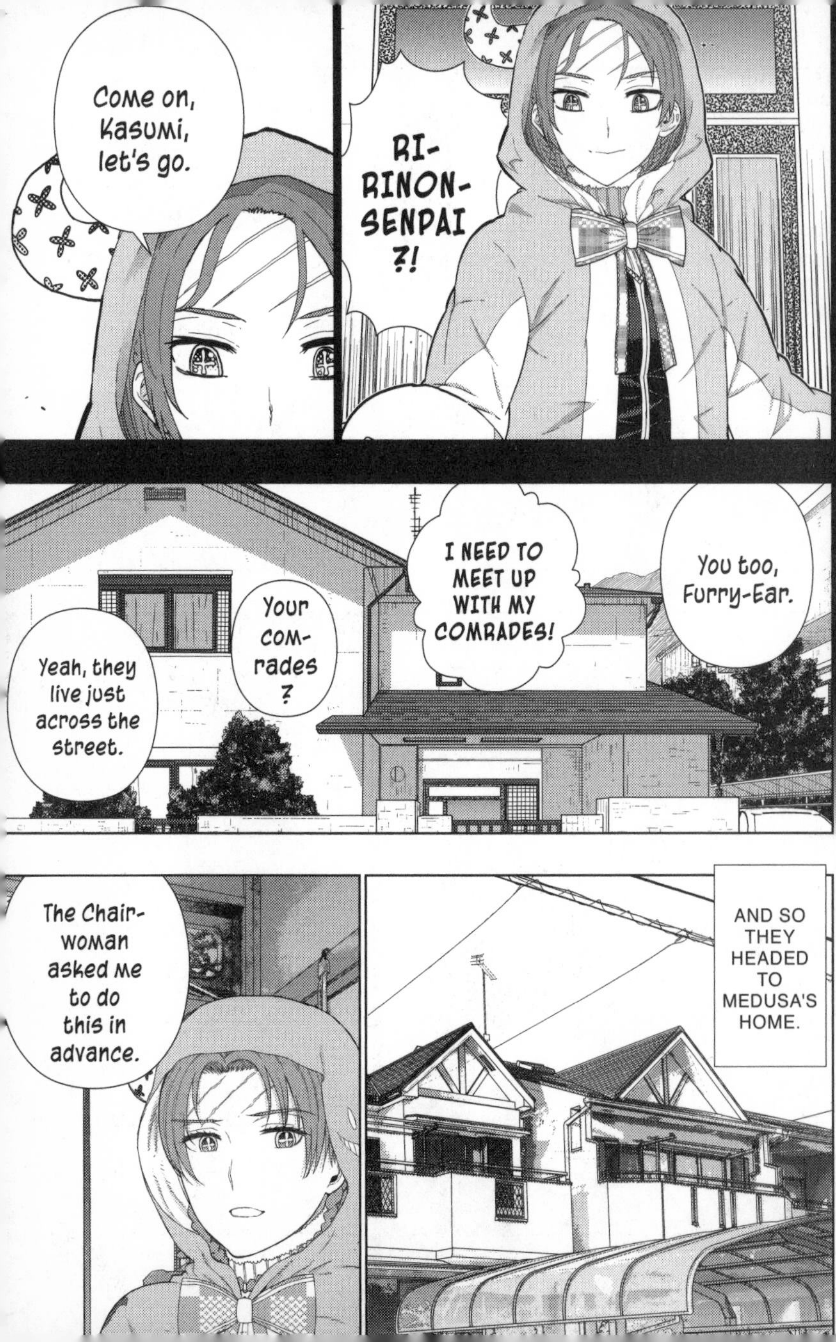
RI-RINON-SENPAI?!
Come on, Kasumi, let's go.
You too, Furry-Ear.
I NEED TO MEET UP WITH MY COMRADES!
Your comrades?
Yeah, they live just across the street.
AND SO THEY HEADED TO MEDUSA'S HOME.
The Chair-woman asked me to do this in advance.

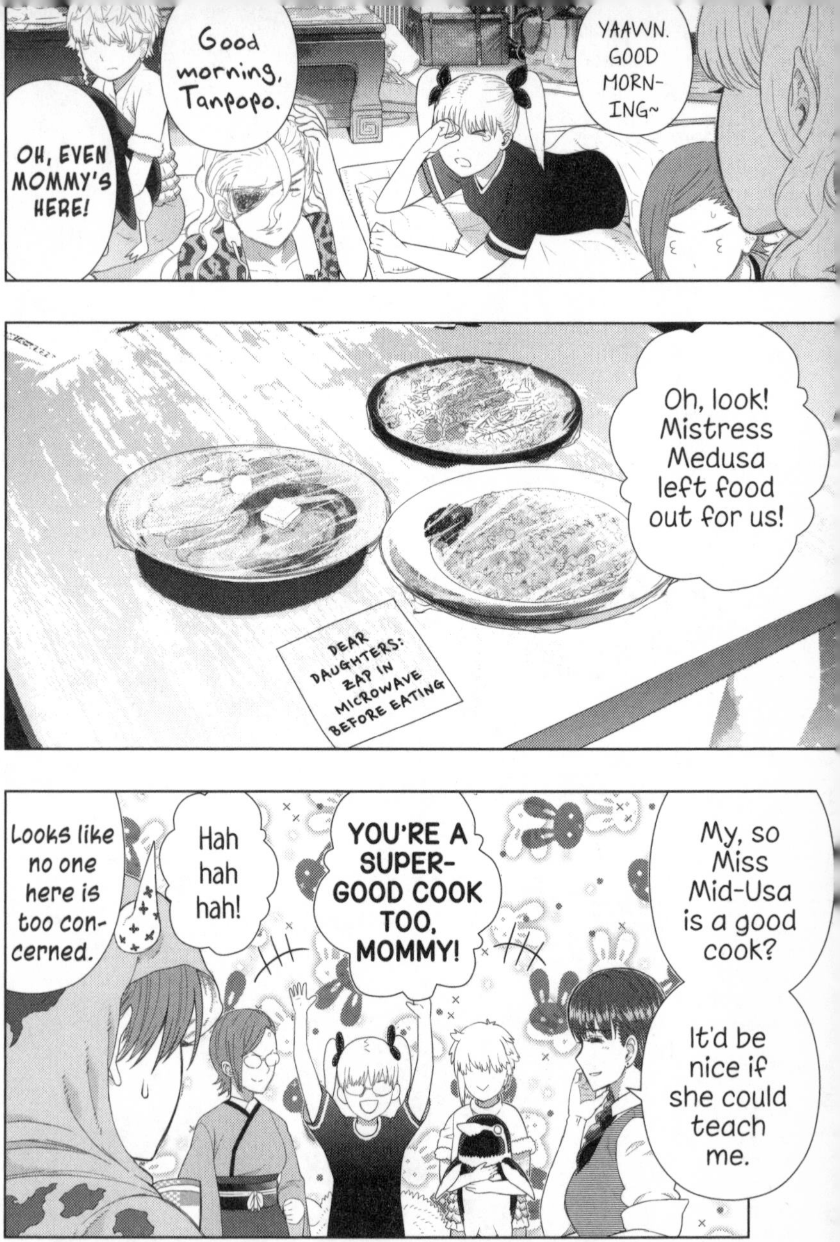

YAAWN. GOOD MORN-ING~
Good morning, Tanpopo.
OH, EVEN MOMMY'S HERE!
Oh, look! Mistress Medusa left food out for us!
DEAR DAUGHTERS: ZAP IN MICROWAVE BEFORE EATING
My, so Miss Mid-Usa is a good cook?
It'd be nice if she could teach me.
YOU'RE A SUPER-GOOD COOK TOO, MOMMY!
Hah hah hah!
Looks like no one here is too con-cerned.

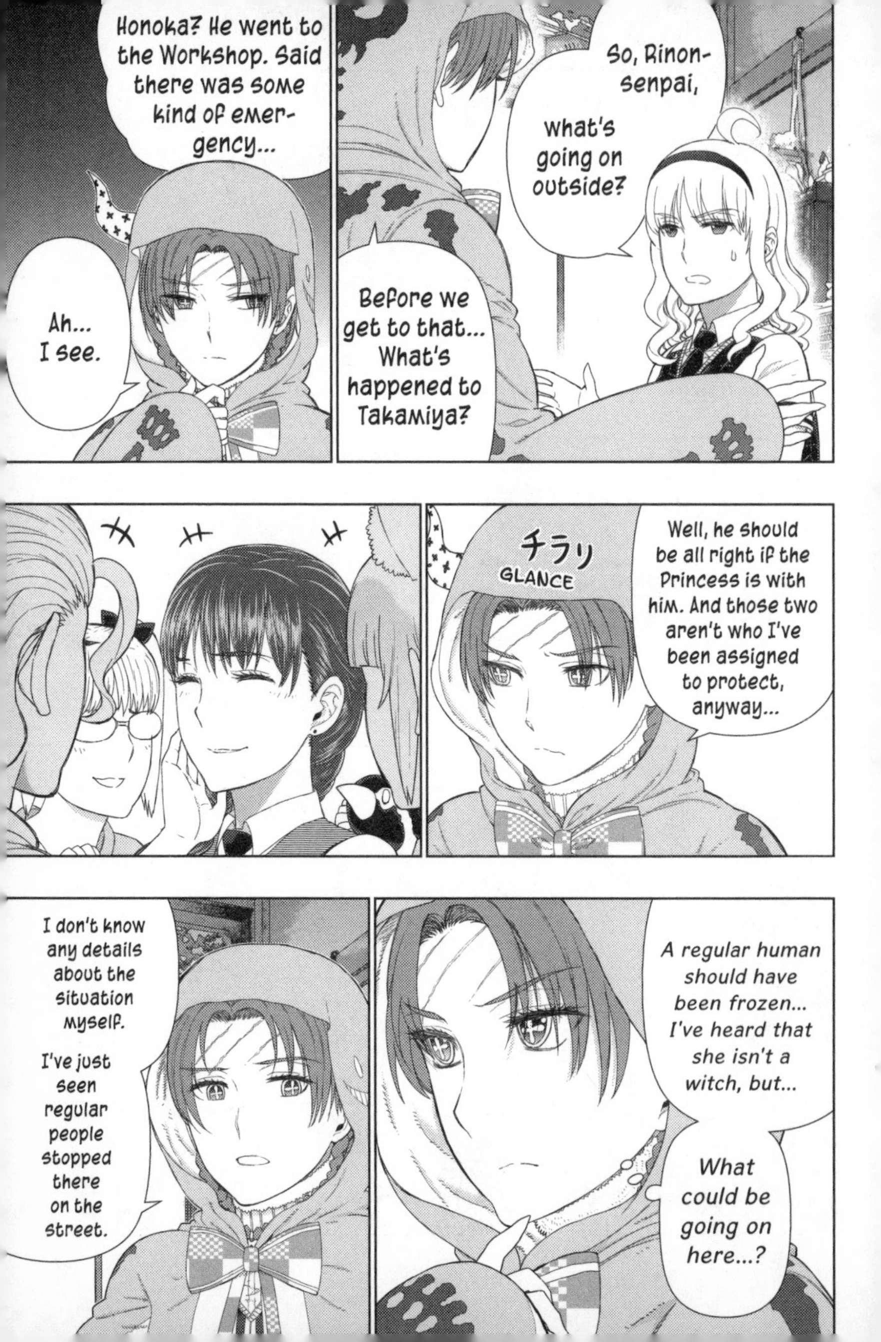
So, Rinon-senpai, what's going on outside?
Before we get to that... What's happened to Takamiya?
Honoka? He went to the Workshop. Said there was some kind of emergency...
Ah... I see.
チラリ
GLANCE
Well, he should be all right if the Princess is with him. And those two aren't who I've been assigned to protect, anyway...
A regular human should have been frozen... I've heard that she isn't a witch, but...
What could be going on here...?
I don't know any details about the situation myself.
I've just seen regular people stopped there on the street.

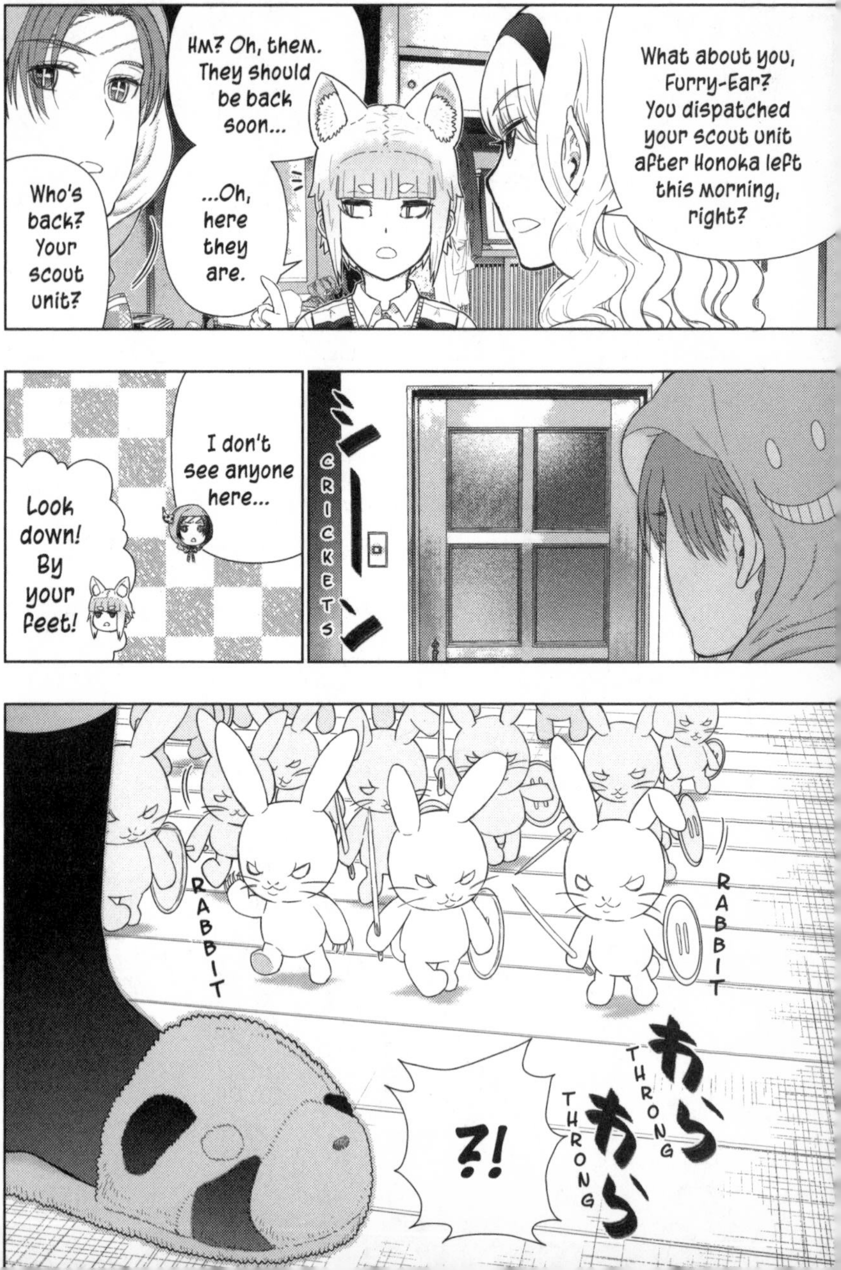
What about you, Furry-Ear? You dispatched your scout unit after Honoka left this morning, right?
Hm? Oh, them. They should be back soon...
Who's back? Your scout unit?
...Oh, here they are.
CRICKETS
I don't see anyone here...
Look down! By your feet!
RABBIT
RABBIT
THRONG
THRONG
?!

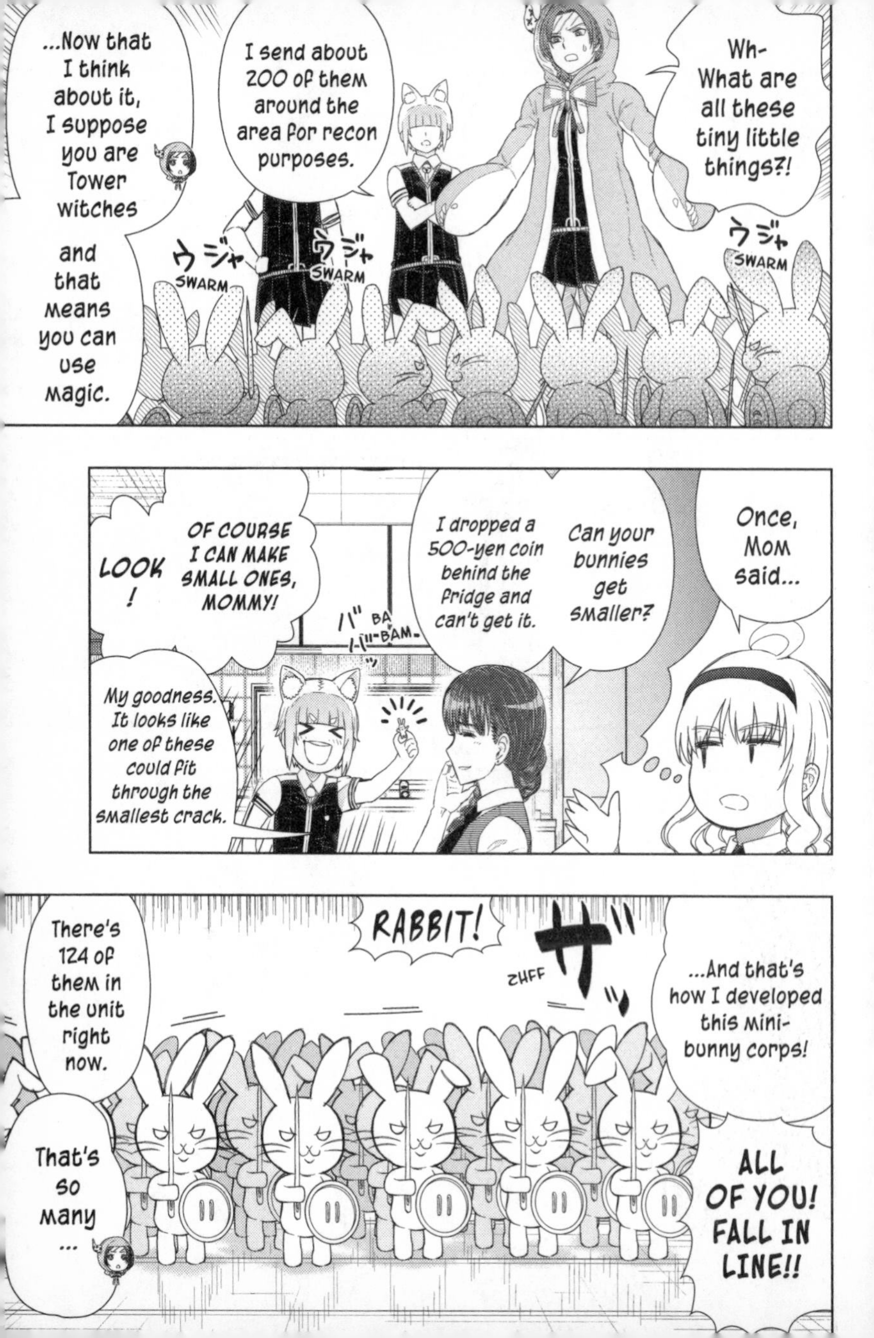
Wh- What are all these tiny little things?!
ウジャ SWARM
I send about 200 of them around the area for recon purposes.
ウジャ SWARM
ウジャ SWARM
...Now that I think about it, I suppose you are Tower witches
and that means you can use magic.
Once, Mom said...
Can your bunnies get smaller?
I dropped a 500-yen coin behind the fridge and can't get it.
バババッ BA-BAM
OF COURSE I CAN MAKE SMALL ONES, MOMMY!
LOOK!
My goodness. It looks like one of these could fit through the smallest crack.
...And that's how I developed this mini-bunny corps!
ALL OF YOU! FALL IN LINE!!
ザッ ZHFF
RABBIT!
There's 124 of them in the unit right now.
That's so many...

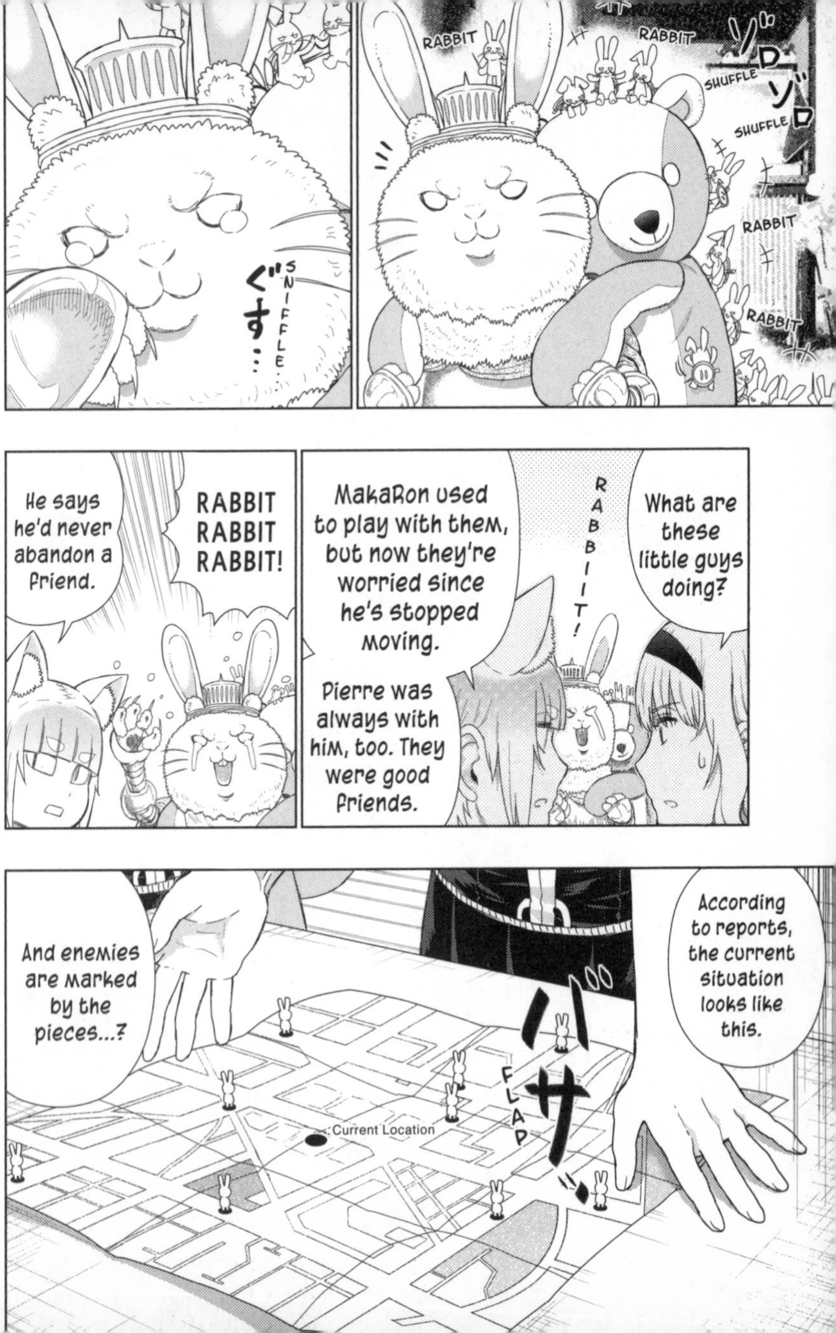
RABBIT
RABBIT
ゾロゾロ
SHUFFLE
SHUFFLE
RABBIT
RABBIT
ぐす…
SNIFFLE…
What are these little guys doing?
RABBIT!
MakaRon used to play with them, but now they're worried since he's stopped moving.
Pierre was always with him, too. They were good friends.
RABBIT RABBIT RABBIT!
He says he'd never abandon a friend.
According to reports, the current situation looks like this.
ハサ
FLAP
Current Location
And enemies are marked by the pieces…?

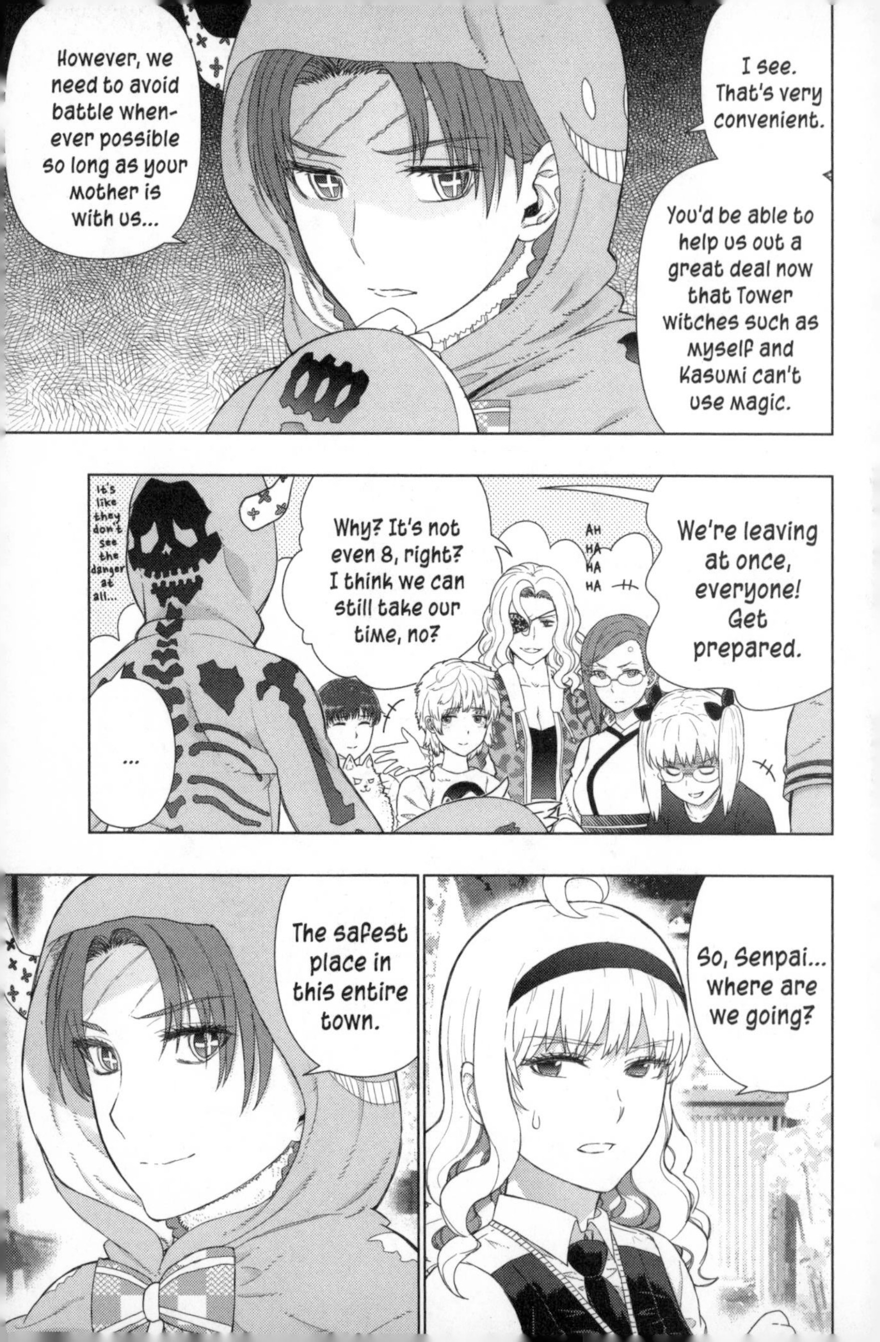
I see. That's very convenient.
You'd be able to help us out a great deal now that Tower witches such as myself and Kasumi can't use magic.
However, we need to avoid battle whenever possible so long as your mother is with us...
We're leaving at once, everyone! Get prepared.
AH HA HA HA
Why? It's not even 8, right? I think we can still take our time, no?
It's like they don't see the danger at all...
...
So, Senpai... where are we going?
The safest place in this entire town.

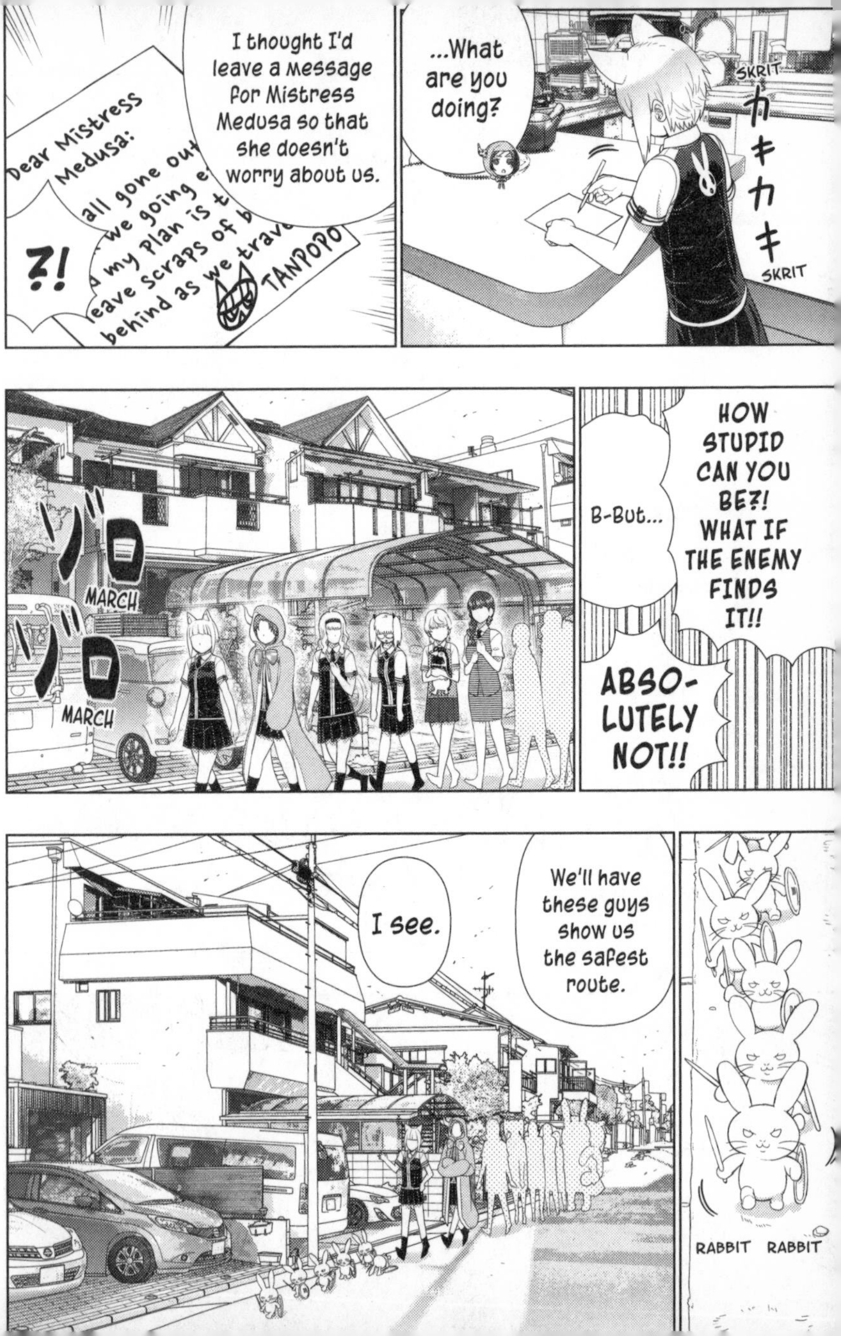
...What are you doing?
カキカキ
SKRIT
SKRIT
I thought I'd leave a message for Mistress Medusa so that she doesn't worry about us.
Dear Mistress Medusa:
all gone out
we going e
my plan is t
leave scraps of b
behind as we trave
TANPOPO
?!
HOW STUPID CAN YOU BE?! WHAT IF THE ENEMY FINDS IT!!
B-But...
ABSO-LUTELY NOT!!
MARCH
MARCH
RABBIT RABBIT
We'll have these guys show us the safest route.
I see.

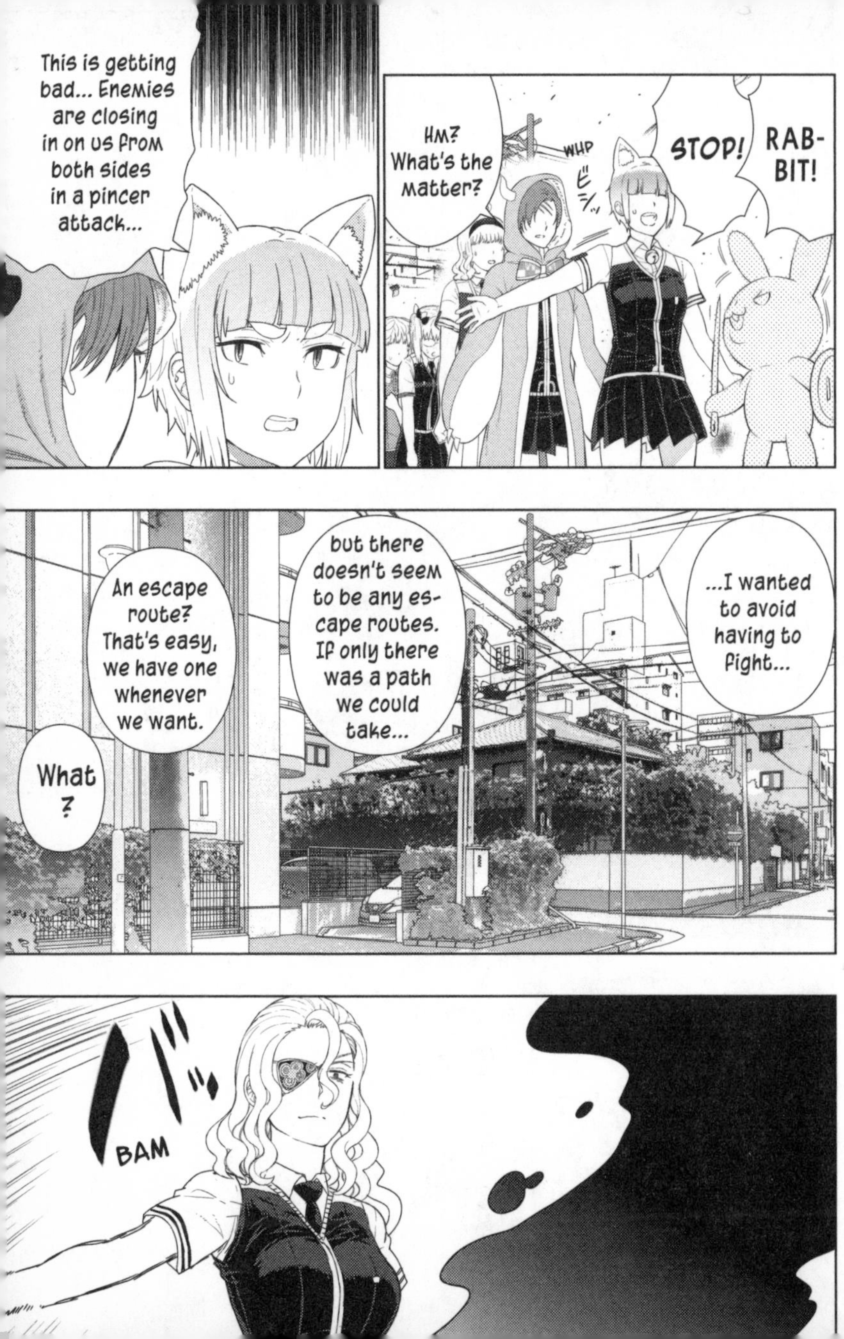
RAB-BIT!
STOP!
WHP
Hm? What's the matter?
This is getting bad... Enemies are closing in on us from both sides in a pincer attack...
...I wanted to avoid having to fight...
but there doesn't seem to be any es-cape routes. If only there was a path we could take...
An escape route? That's easy, we have one whenever we want.
What?
BAM

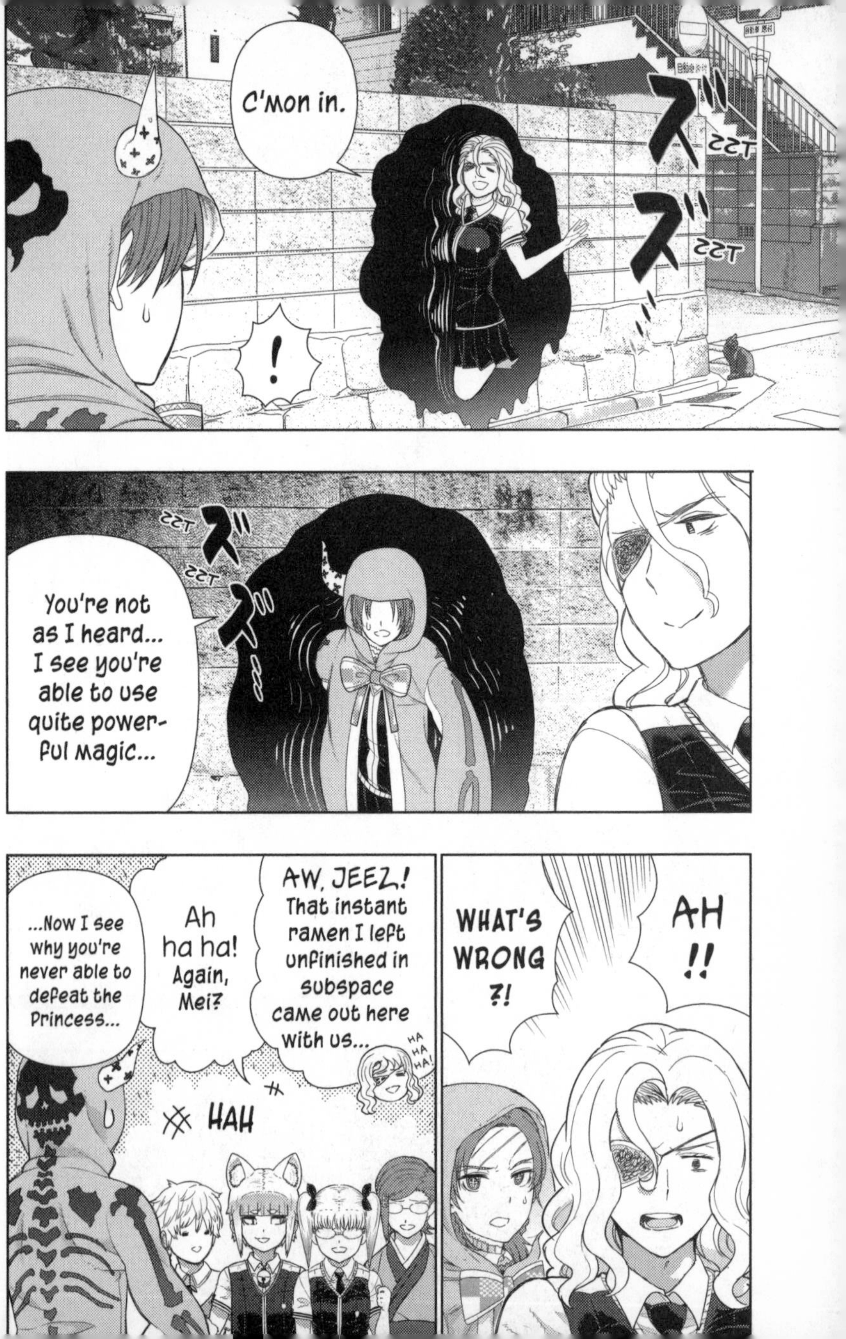

ZZT
ZZT
C'mon in.
!
ZZT
ZZT
You're not as I heard... I see you're able to use quite power-ful magic...
AH !!
WHAT'S WRONG ?!
AW, JEEZ! That instant ramen I left unfinished in subspace came out here with us...
HA HA HA!
Ah ha ha! Again, Mei?
...Now I see why you're never able to defeat the Princess...
HAH

ザ RUSTLE
ザ RUSTLE

ズン THOOM

Shh! Be quiet... Stop moving.

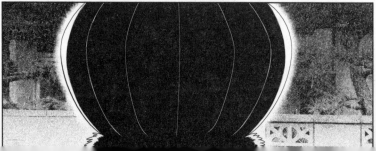

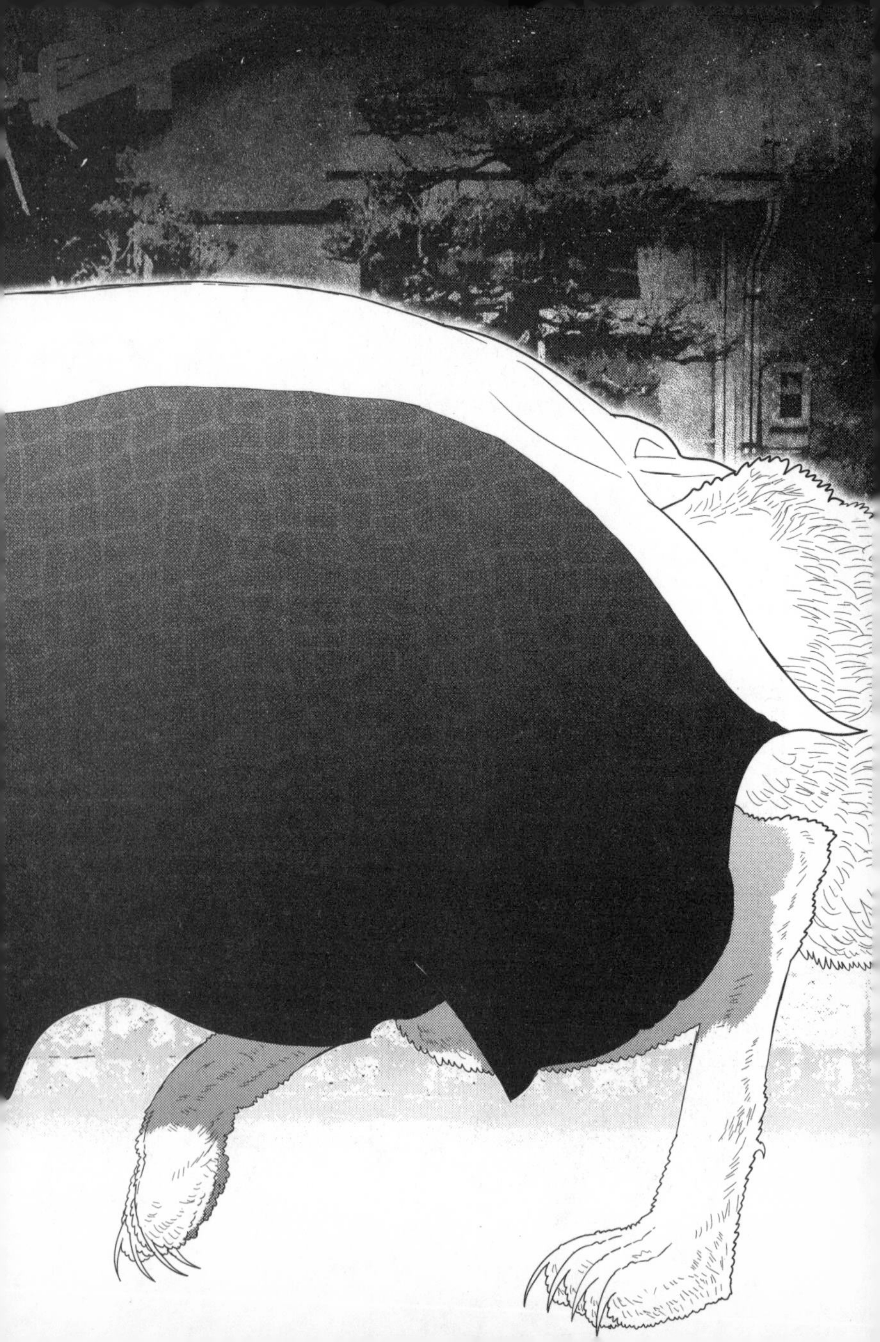

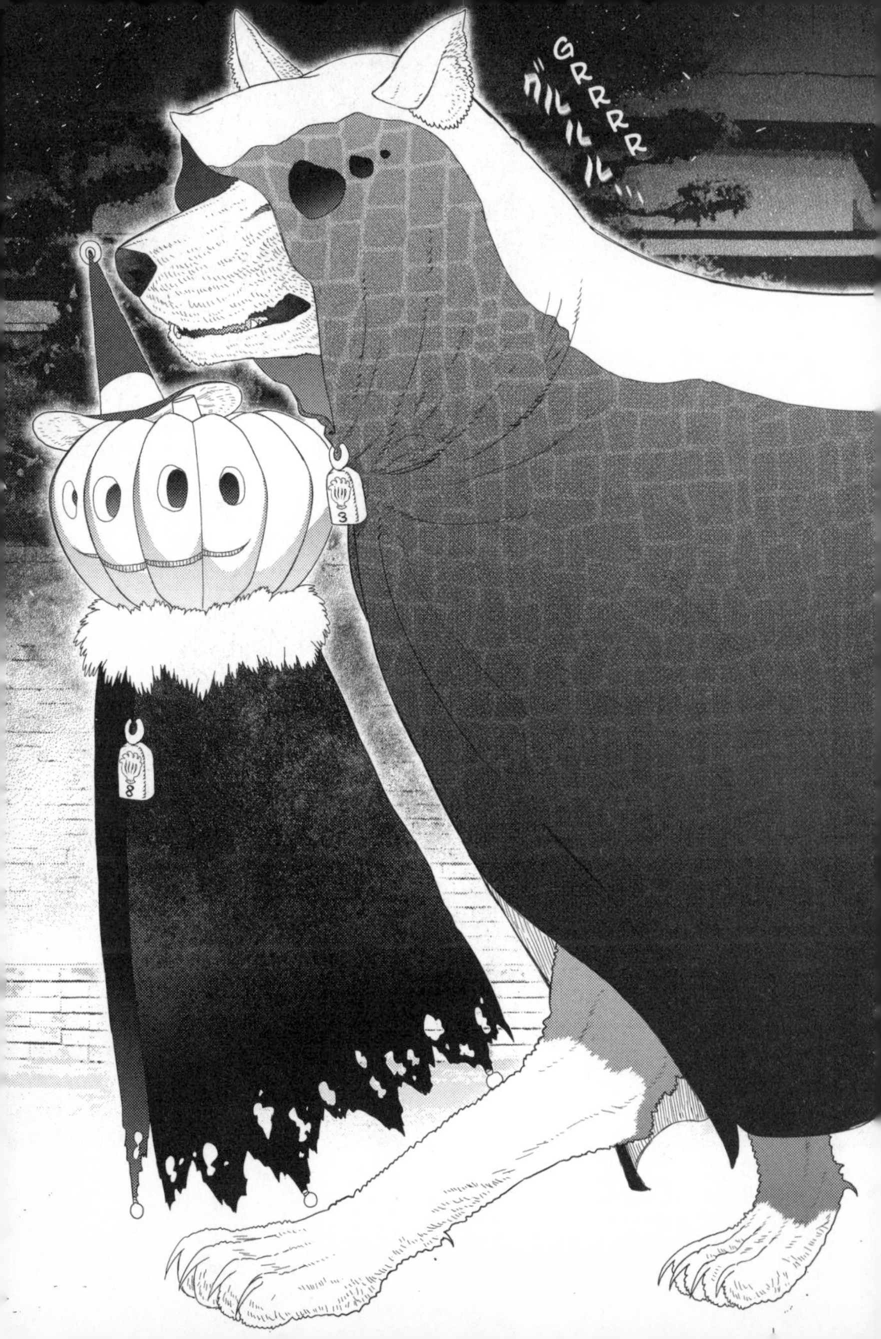
GRRRR
ガルルル

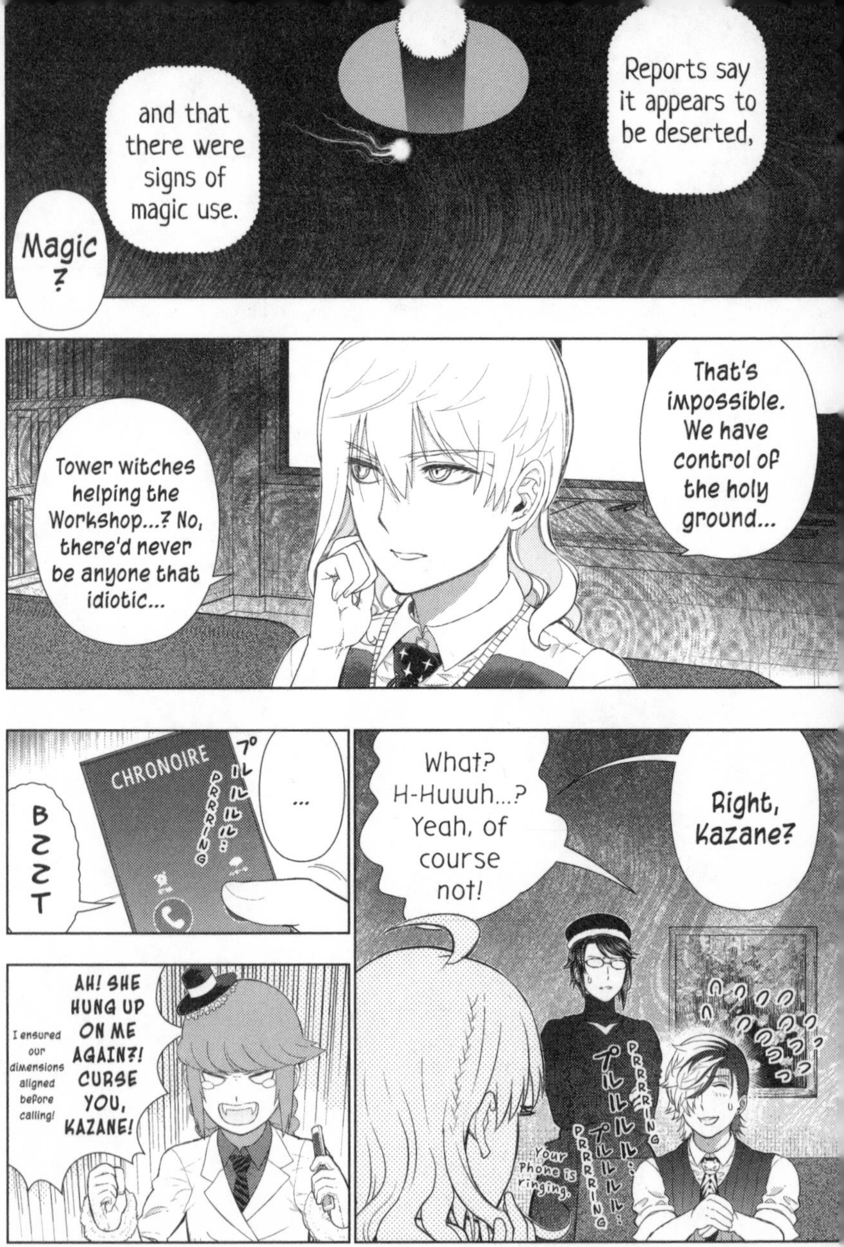
Reports say it appears to be deserted,
and that there were signs of magic use.
Magic?
That's impossible. We have control of the holy ground...
Tower witches helping the Workshop...? No, there'd never be anyone that idiotic...
Right, Kazane?
What? H-Huuuh...? Yeah, of course not!
PRRRRING
PRRRRING
Your Phone is ringing.
...
CHRONOIRE
PRRRING
BZZT
AH! SHE HUNG UP ON ME AGAIN?! CURSE YOU, KAZANE!
I ensured our dimensions aligned before calling!

Witchcraft Works

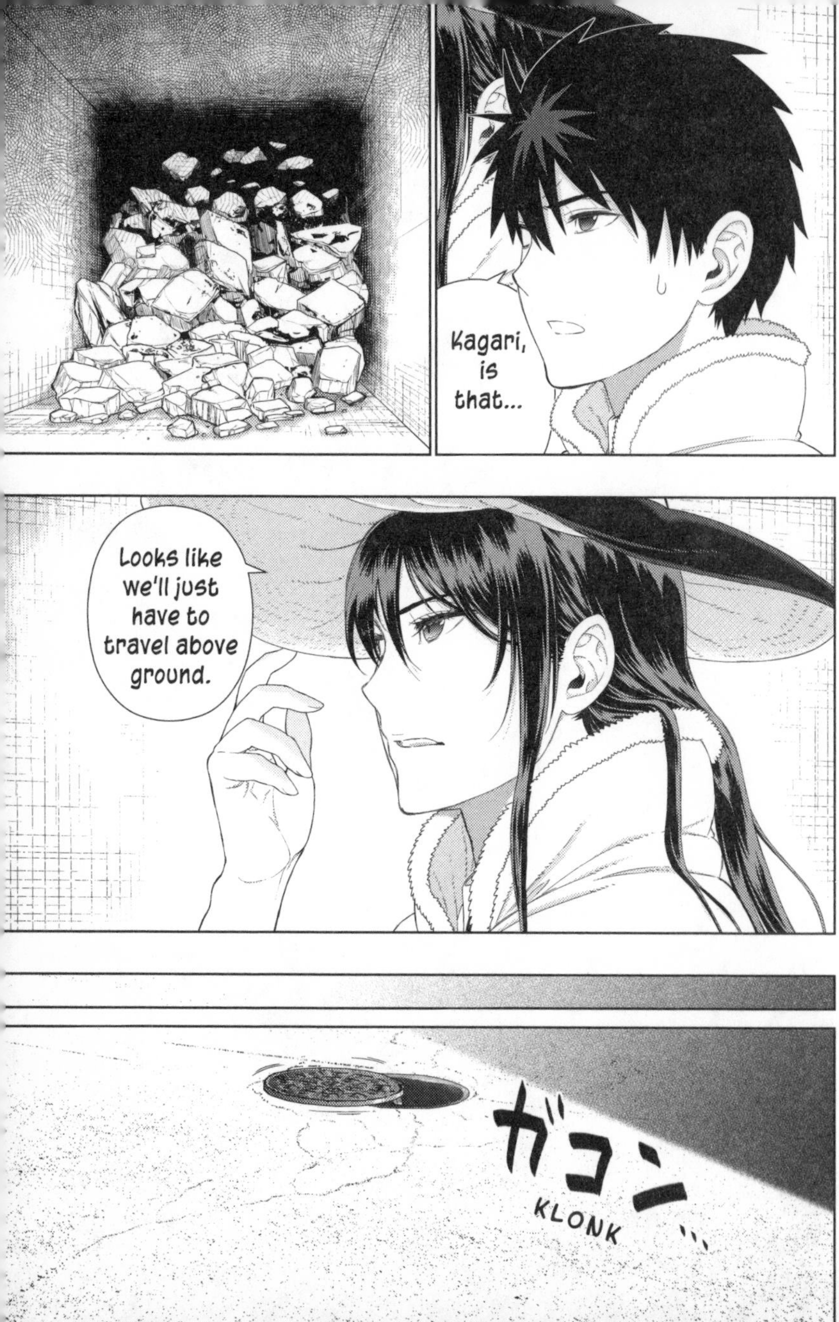
Kagari, is that...
Looks like we'll just have to travel above ground.
ガコン
KLONK

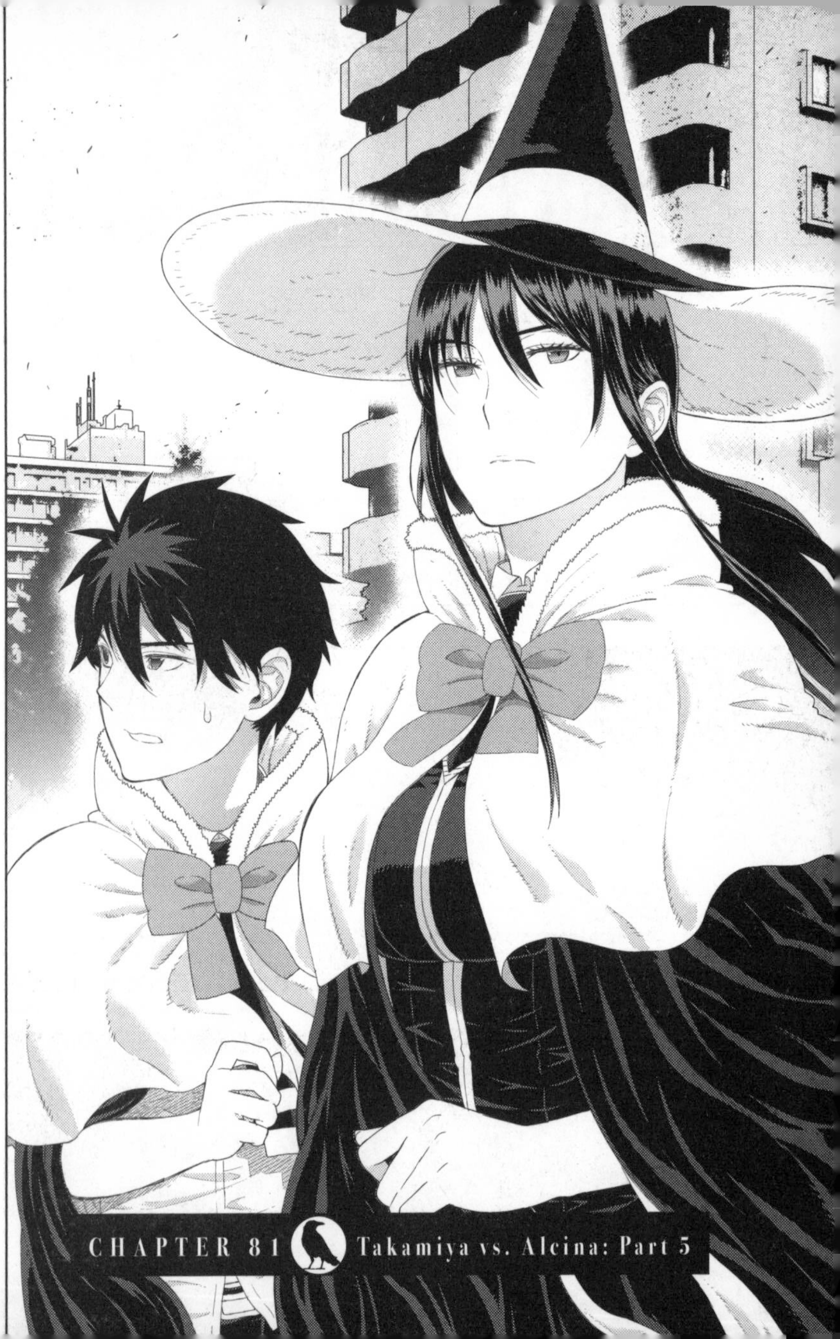

CHAPTER 81 Takamiya vs. Alcina: Part 5

...

Senpai?

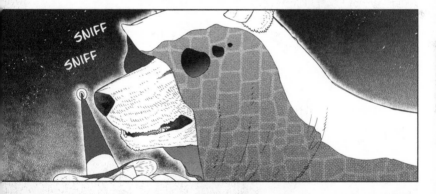

SNIFF
SNIFF

THOOM
HMPH

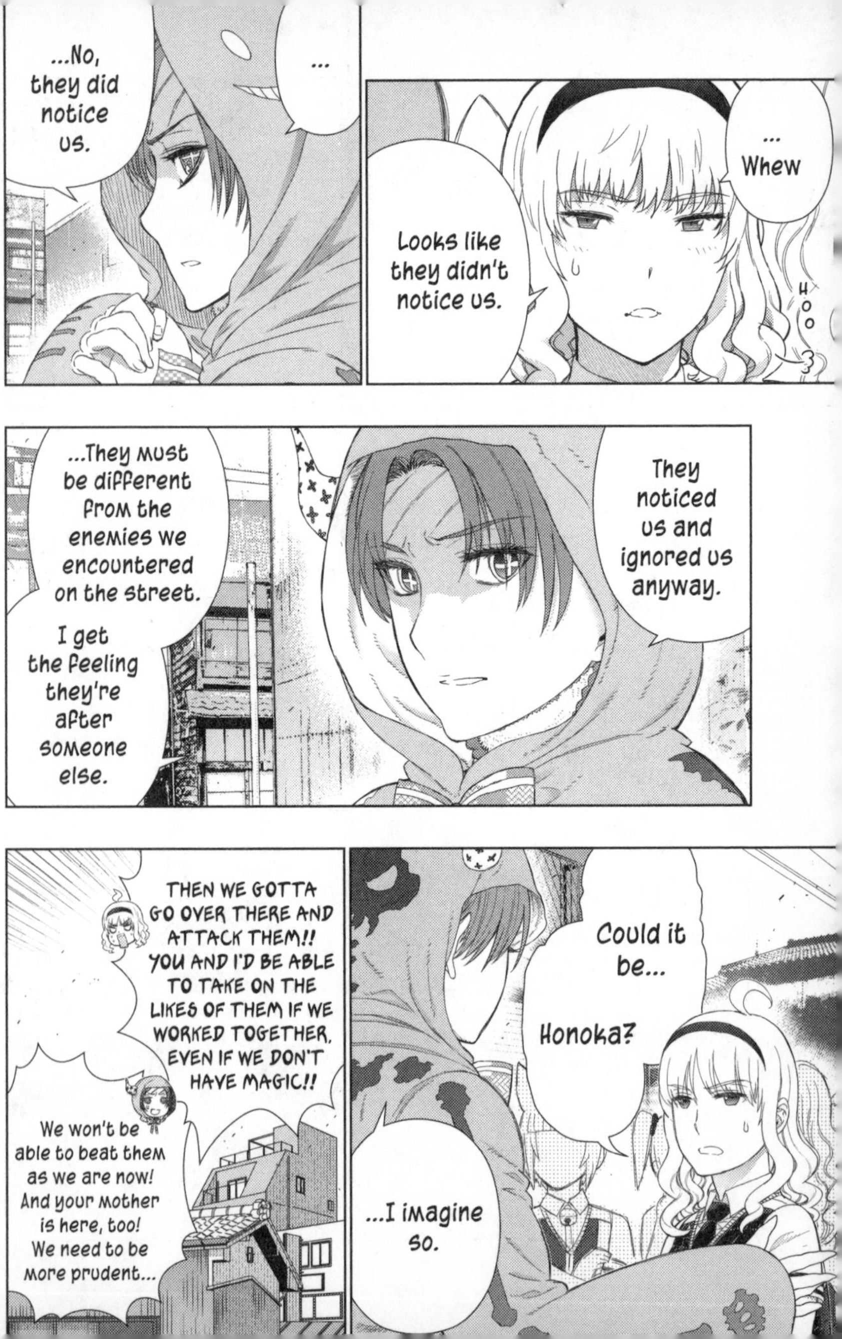
... Whew
Looks like they didn't notice us.
HOO
...
...No, they did notice us.
They noticed us and ignored us anyway.
...They must be different from the enemies we encountered on the street.
I get the feeling they're after someone else.
Could it be... Honoka?
...I imagine so.
THEN WE GOTTA GO OVER THERE AND ATTACK THEM!! YOU AND I'D BE ABLE TO TAKE ON THE LIKES OF THEM IF WE WORKED TOGETHER, EVEN IF WE DON'T HAVE MAGIC!!
We won't be able to beat them as we are now! And your mother is here, too! We need to be more prudent...

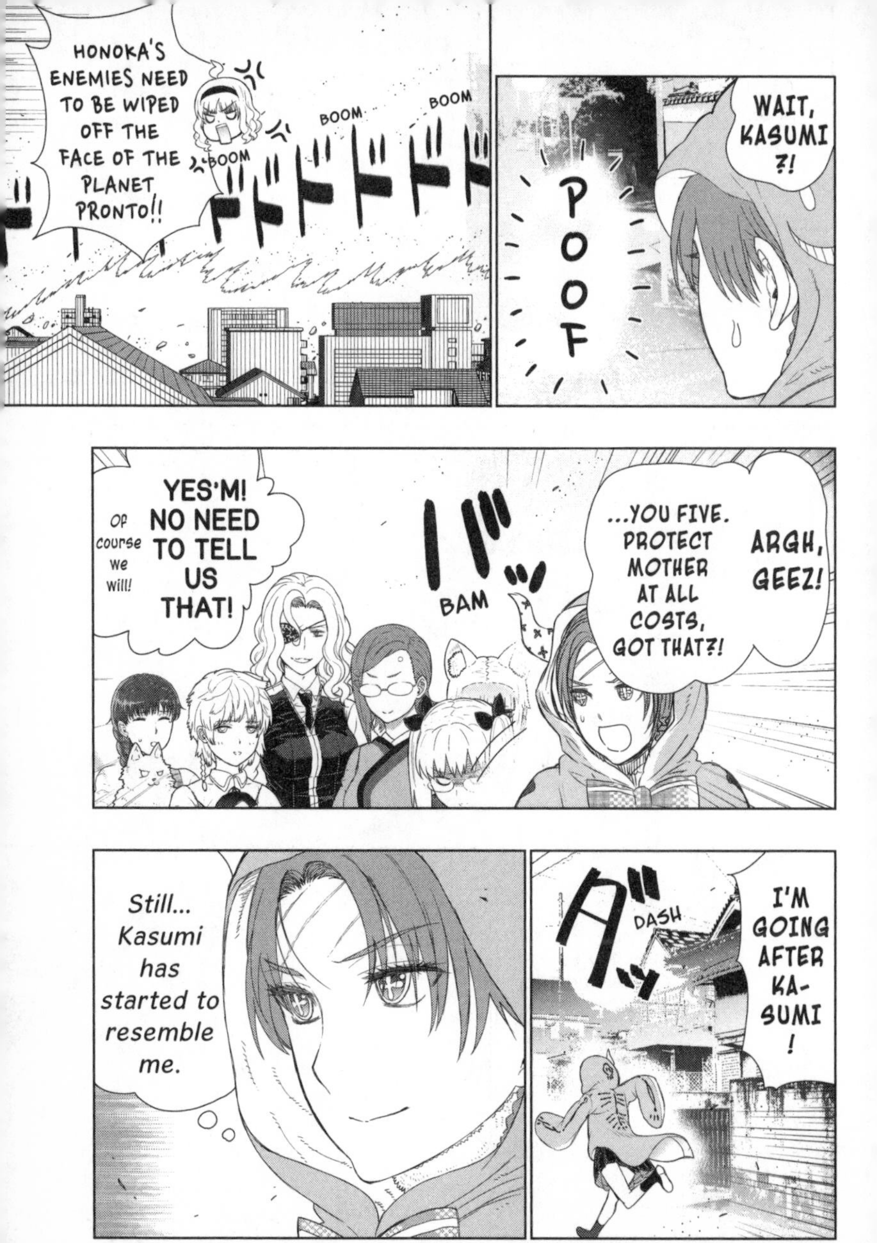
WAIT, KASUMI ?!
POOF
HONOKA'S ENEMIES NEED TO BE WIPED OFF THE FACE OF THE PLANET PRONTO!!
BOOM
BOOM
BOOM
ARGH, GEEZ!
...YOU FIVE. PROTECT MOTHER AT ALL COSTS, GOT THAT?!
BAM
YES'M! NO NEED TO TELL US THAT!
Of course we will!
I'M GOING AFTER KA-SUMI!
DASH
Still... Kasumi has started to resemble me.

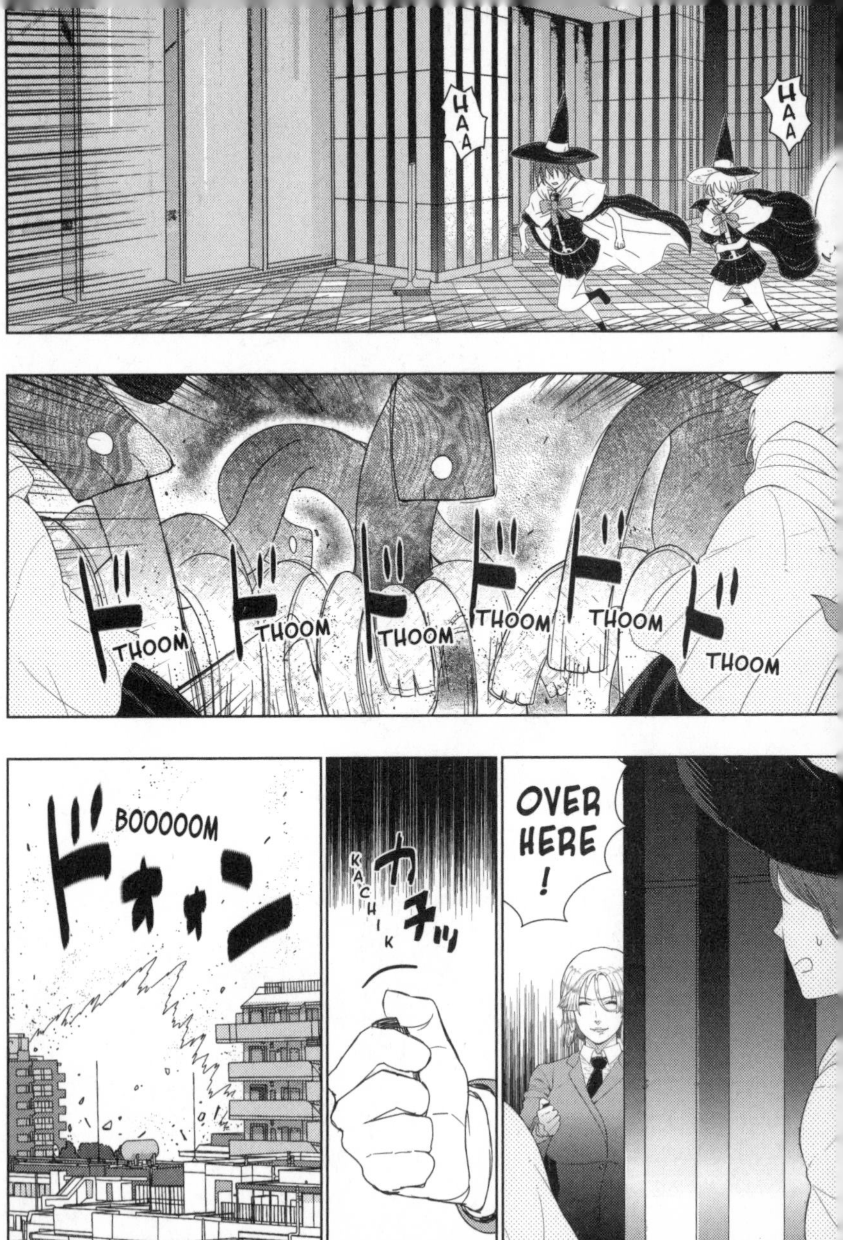
HAA
HAA
ド THOOM
ド THOOM
ド THOOM
ド THOOM
ド THOOM
ド THOOM
OVER HERE !
カチッ KACHIK
ドォォン BOOOOOM

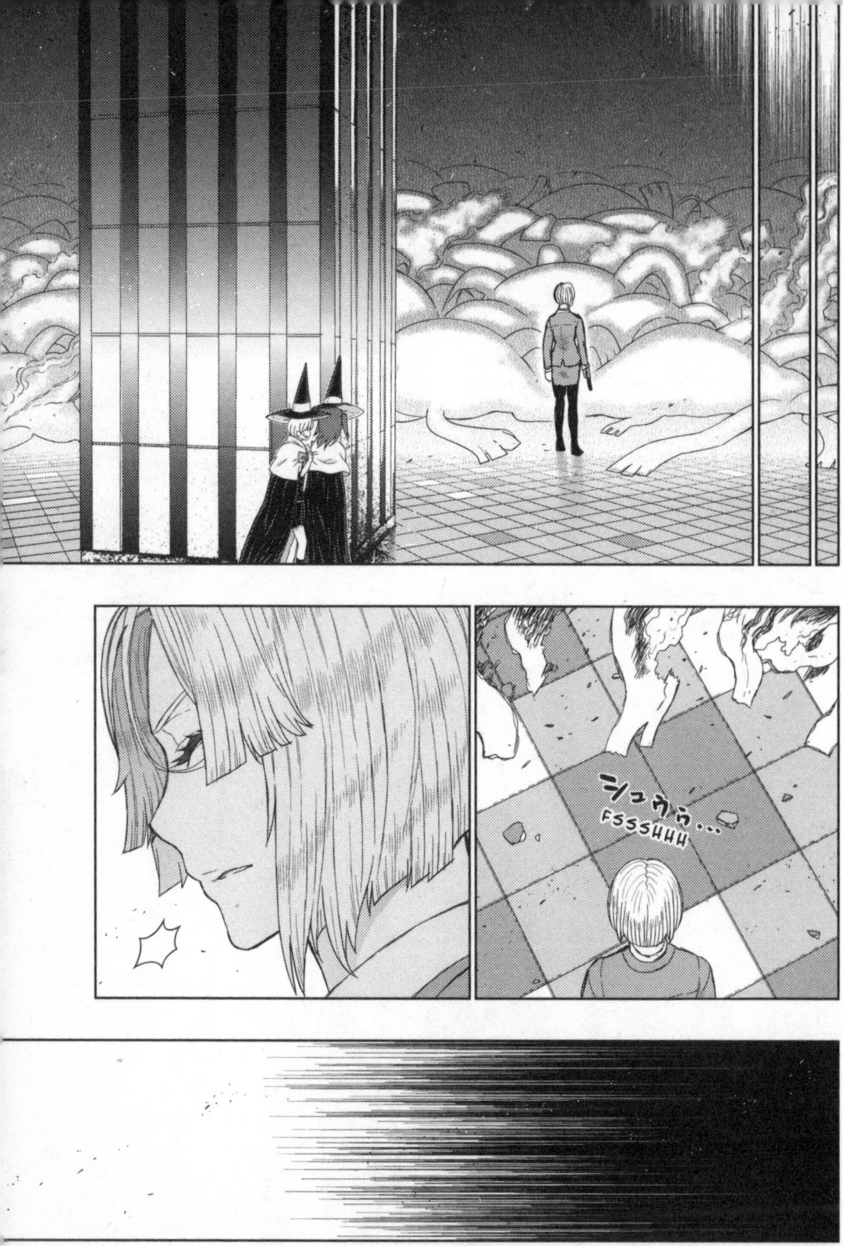
シュウゥ…
FSSSHHH

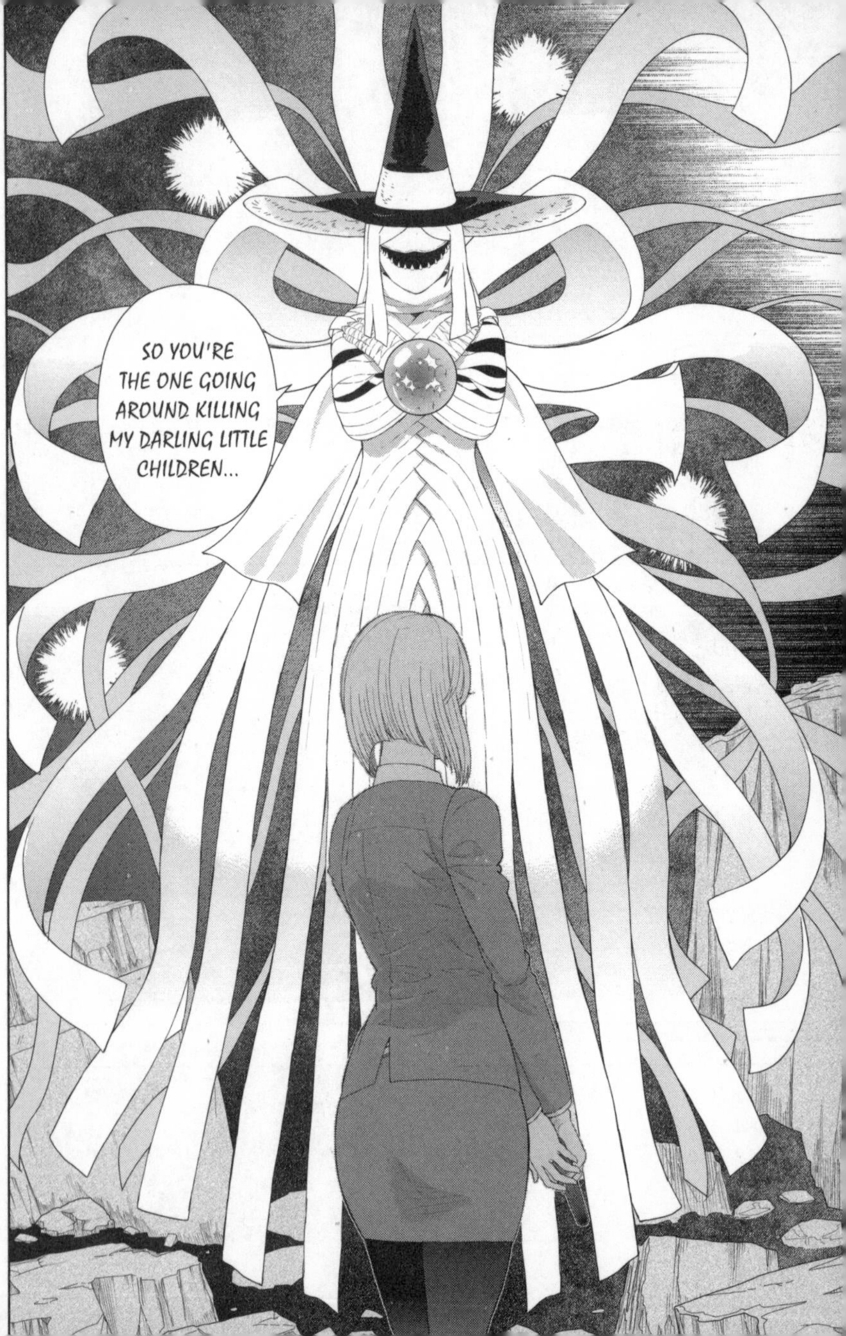
SO YOU'RE THE ONE GOING AROUND KILLING MY DARLING LITTLE CHILDREN...

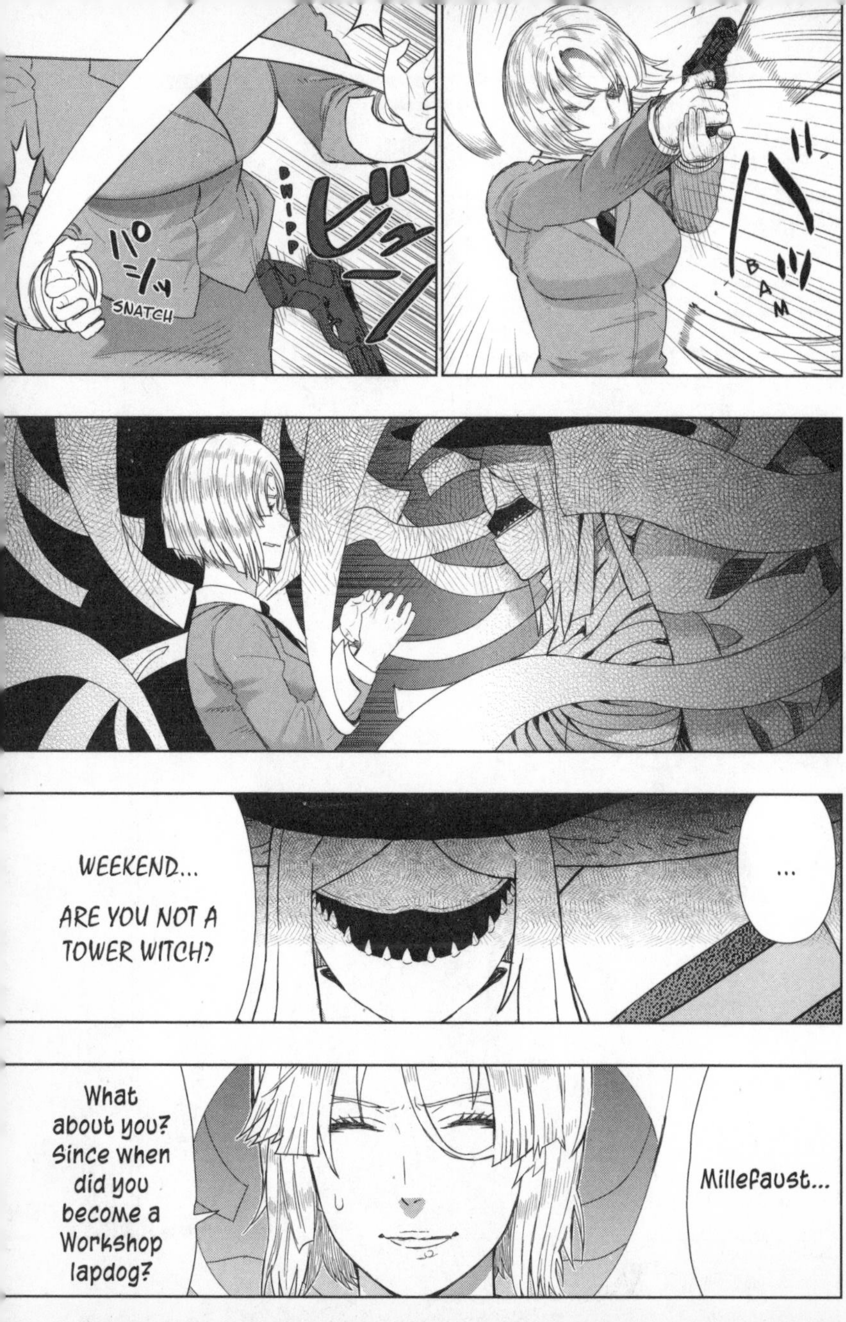
BAM
BWIPP
SNATCH
...
WEEKEND...
ARE YOU NOT A TOWER WITCH?
Millefaust...
What about you? Since when did you become a Workshop lapdog?

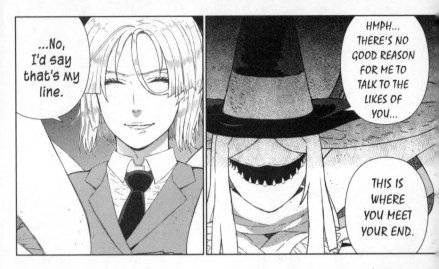

HMPH... THERE'S NO GOOD REASON FOR ME TO TALK TO THE LIKES OF YOU...
THIS IS WHERE YOU MEET YOUR END.
...No, I'd say that's my line.
KACHIK
ゴ
GWOOSH

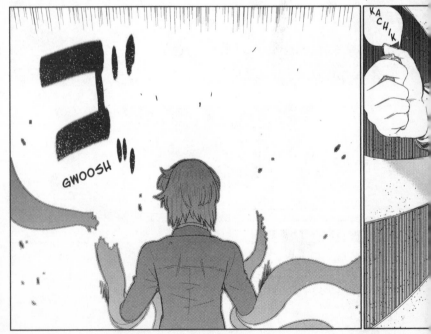

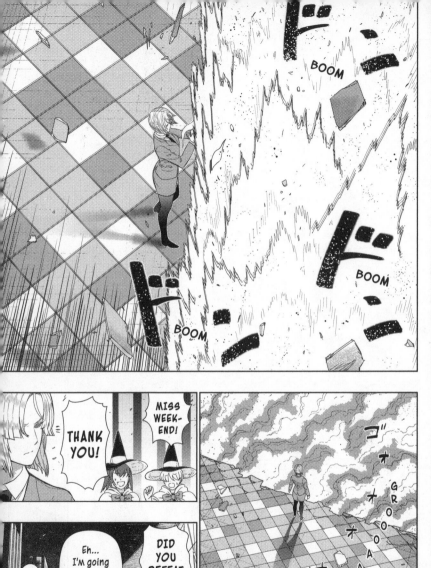

BOOM
BOOM
BOOM
GROOOAAAAR
MISS WEEK-END!
THANK YOU!
DID YOU DEFEAT HER?!
Eh... I'm going back to the base for now. Follow me.
OKAY ...!

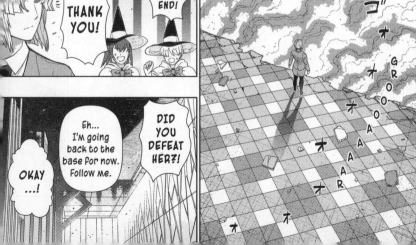

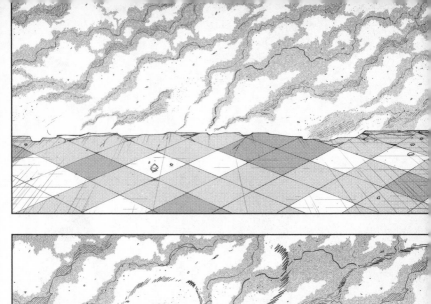

WHOOSH WHOOSH

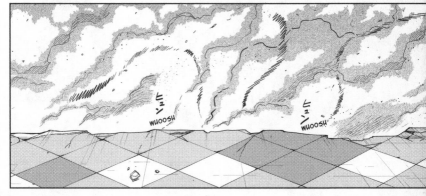

THWAK THWAK THWAK

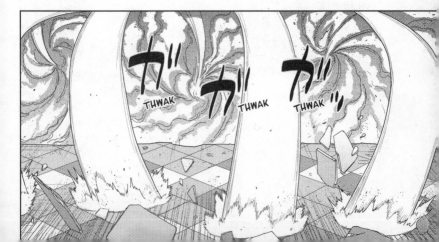

200m先
TOUGETSU CITY CONSUMER CENTER
TOUGETSU CITY CONSUMER CENTER

There doesn't seem to be any enemies around here...

Yeah.

...Um, Kagari?

The whole town being like this... is... all my fault, isn't it?

You've done nothing wrong, Takamiya.
But it's me they're after, right?
So what if that's the case?
All that matters is that you're okay.
...
ZHFF

Ah, there you are.
We found you at last.
THOOOM
GRRR

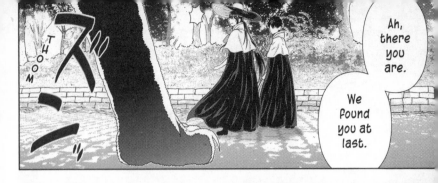

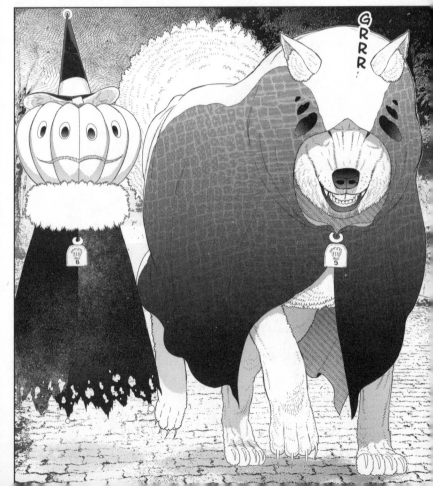

That's right. There are a number of old witches in this town, aren't there?
Chronoire... Medusa... and Kayou...
What about them?
It'd be a nuisance if they got in the way of our actions... so I made a deal with a certain witch,
in exchange for her arms.
ZZSH
OH HO?
THOKK
I SEE YOU'VE ALL GATHERED HERE ALREADY.

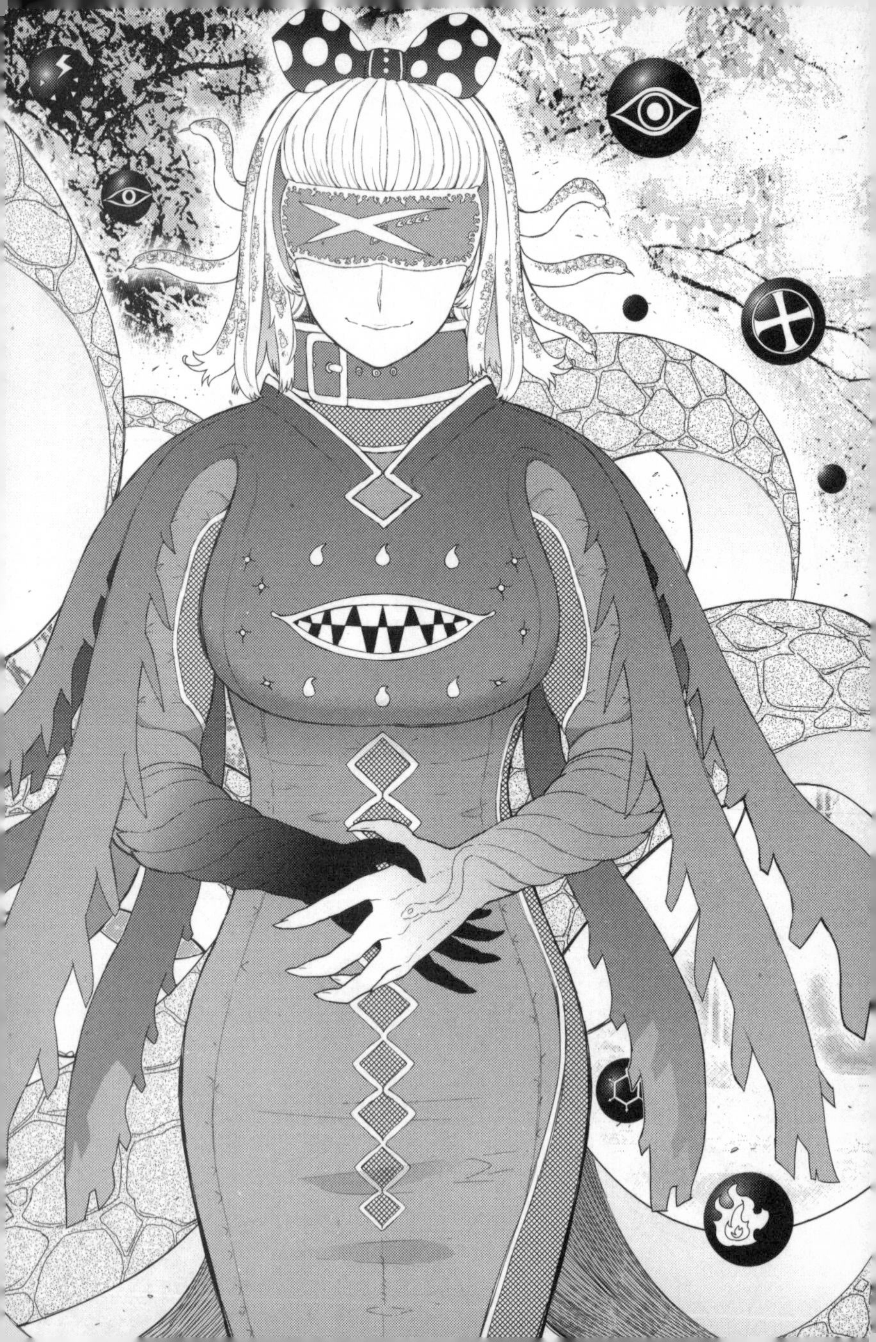

MIND IF I JOIN IN?

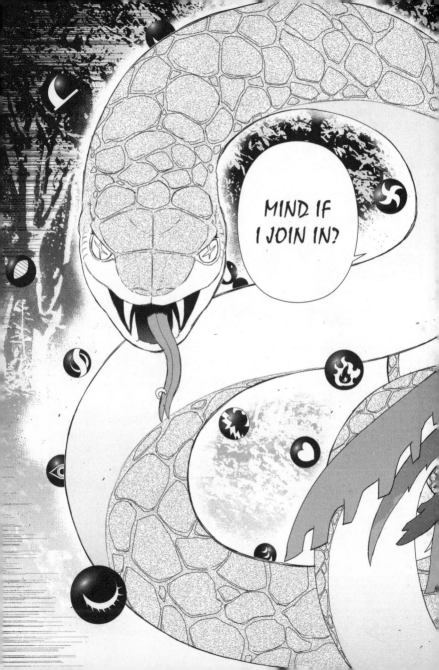

YOU... RECRUITED A TOWER WITCH?!
YOU JUST SAID A PARTNERSHIP WITH THE TOWER WAS UNTHINK-ABLE...!
That's right. Which is why I decided to use the same methods as you.
WHAT METHODS?!
Medusa! We heard you've temporarily become a Workshop witch!
Hmph! I guess they let you inspectors get away with any thing, huh?
...But don't stick your nose in our business! These children are my prey!
You just sit there quietly and watch!

CHAPTER 31 END

Witchcraft Works

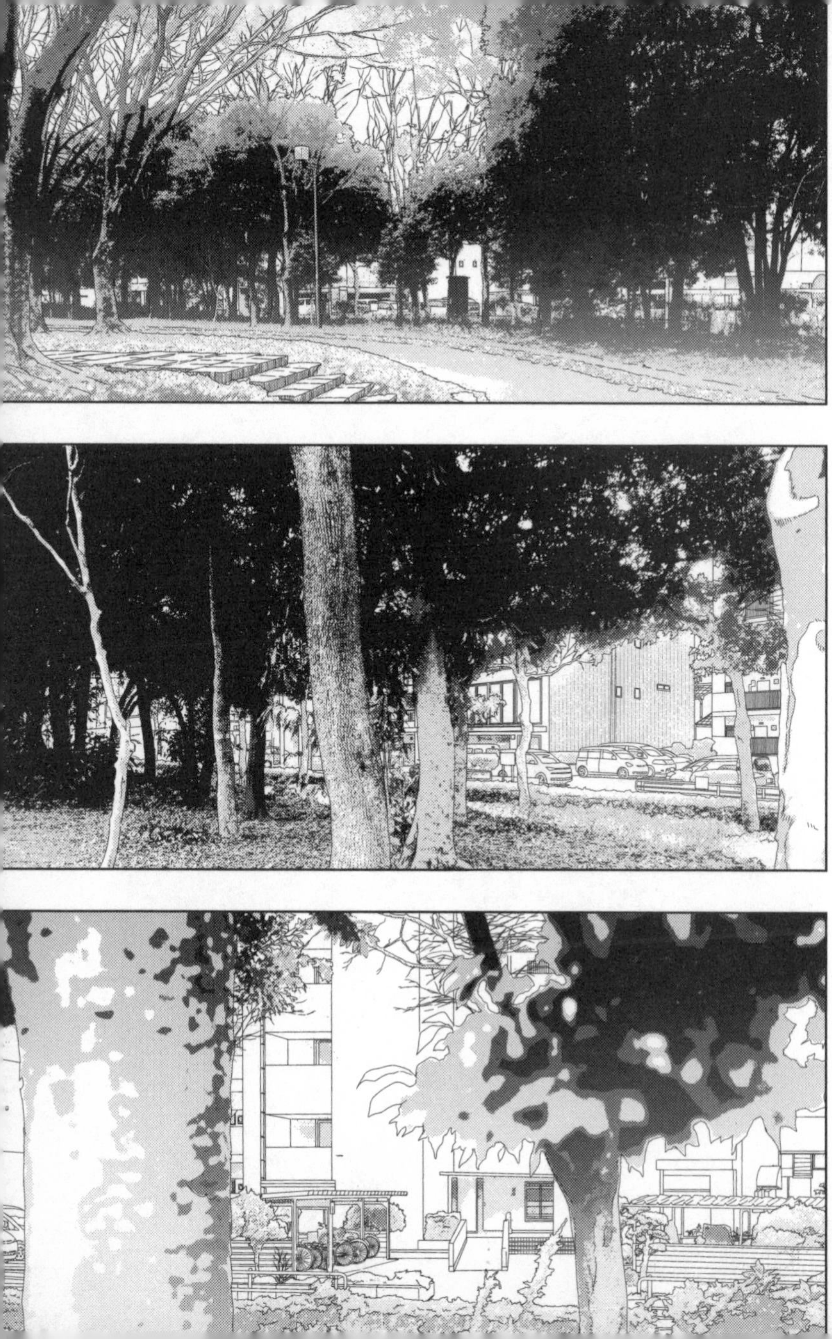

CHAPTER 82 Takamiya vs. Alcina: Part 6

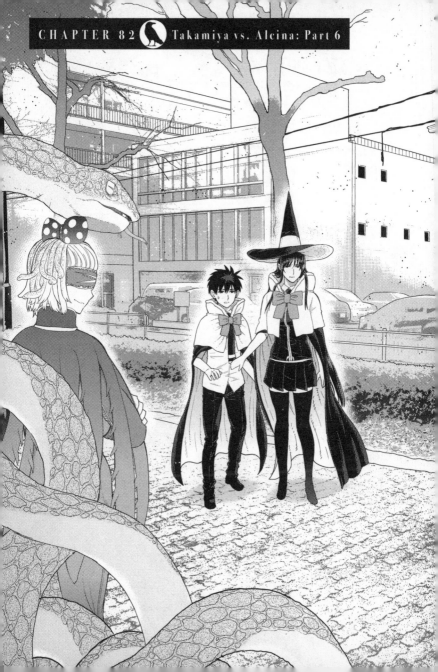

YOU JUST STAY OUT OF THIS!

WE FOUND TAKAMIYA FIRST!

HAH! I'M NOT LETTING YOU MAKE SOME KIND OF RIDICULOUS PROPOSAL TO FIGHT TOGETHER, MEDUSA!

I only wanted to say that I'm not your enemy.

Oh, that's fine with me. I'm not on your side, after all.

Sorry about this, Takamiya— I made a deal with Alcina.

MISS MEDUSA! WHAT'S GOING ON HERE ...?

...A deal?

It seems she's expecting to collect you.
To the point she was willing to bring those sham Craft-users over there known as Hydra Head...
Hey! WHAT DID YOU JUST SAY? DID YOU JUST CALL US SHAMS?!
JUST STAY OUT OF THIS!
...So you did it, Medusa.

You were the one to petrify time in this town and stop everything...

And...you petrified our path to the holy ground, as well as our options along with it.

You led us here...

That was my plan...

but those two over there found you first. I'm surprised at just how good her nose is.

Hmph! HEARING PRAISE FROM YOU DOESN'T MAKE ME THE LEAST BIT HAPPY!

...

All right, enough prattle!

THOOM ズン

...I am Burrowsdate of Hydra Head!

So. The White Princess's host and his knight...

I've always wanted the chance to eat you.

SWRRR

WRR

WRR

...!
KAGARI
...

B-S-H-T

THOOM

...Don't you smell nice.
Leave some for me, okay?
You look delicious.
DASH
だっ

HAAH !!
I'M PRO-TECTING HONOKA !!!

ド
BA
ゴォ
THWAK

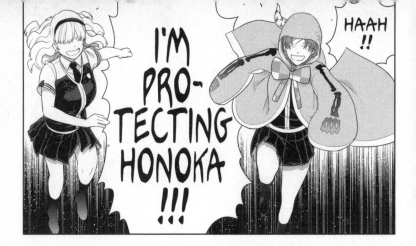

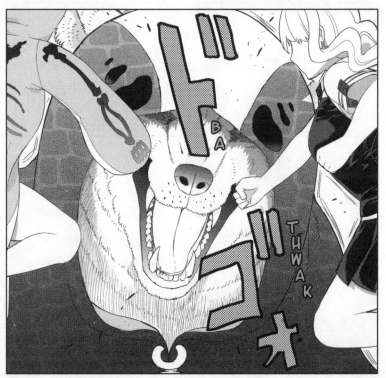

...

OWWWWWW! SHE'S SUPER HARD!!

PWOK
PWOK
PWOK

YAAAAH!!

AS IF THAT'D DETER ME!

...Heh. Looks like you're in trouble, Burrows. ♪

...

AH!

CHOMP

SEN-PAAA-AAAA-!!!!!!!!

GULP

HOW DARE YOU DO THAT TO HER!
ばっ
BAM
CALM DOWN, KASUMI!
Hm... So her ability is that of the Iron Fist...
ペロリ
LICK
MY CRAFT IS KNOWN AS THE FOOD CHAIN! I CAN USE THE ABILITIES OF ANY WITCHES I EAT!
...AND I THINK I'LL SHOW IT OFF HERE, JUST FOR YOU!

GAH
ZZZT
ズ
ZZZT
ズ
ZZZT
ズ
ZZZT
ズ
ZZZT
ズ
ZZZT
ズ
ZZZT
ズ

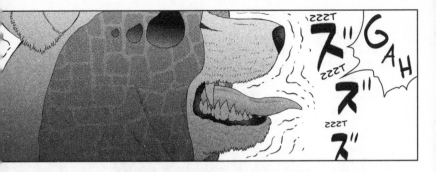

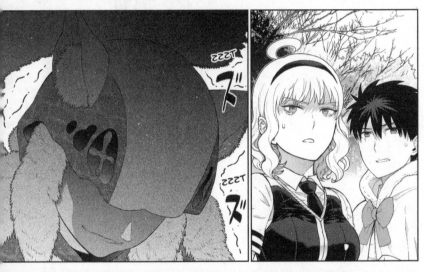

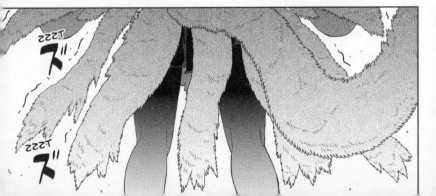

What do you think?
I bet it'll be a lot of fun smashing you up in this form.
GIVE SENPAI BACK!!

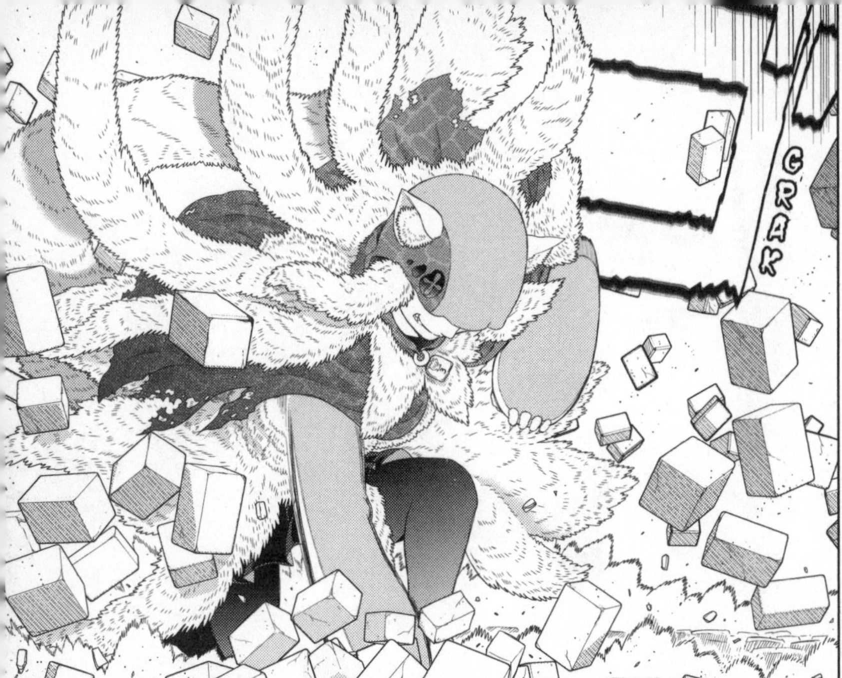
GRAK
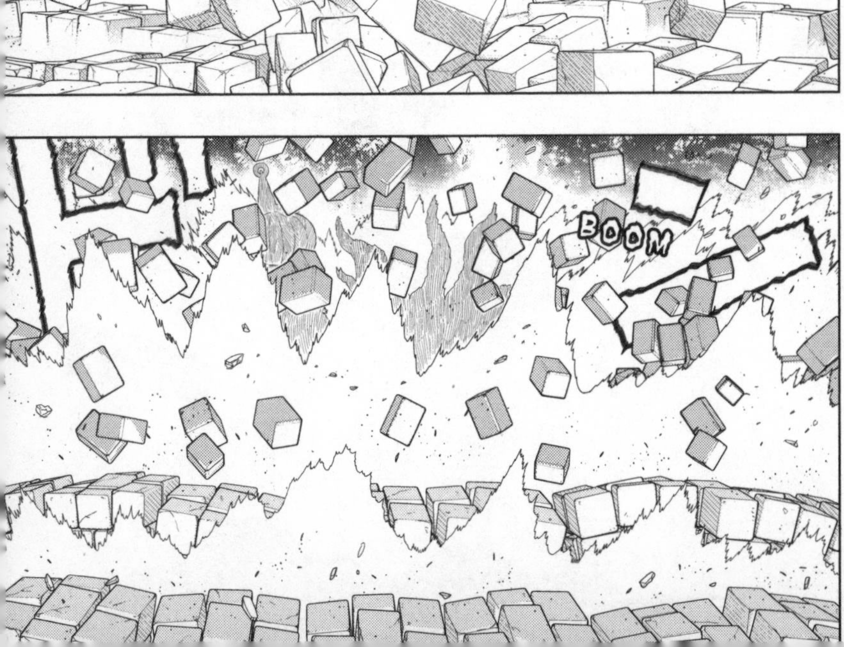
BOOM

BOOM
BOOM

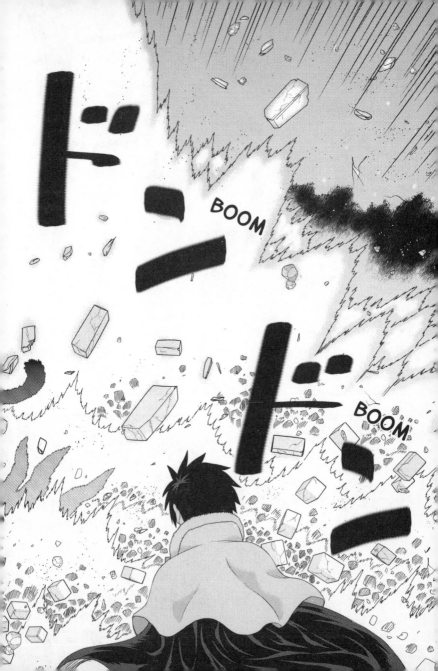

BOOM
ドン

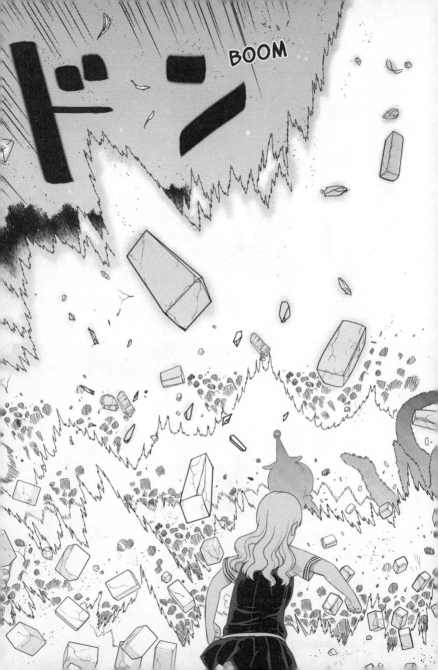

ゴォ
GWOOSH
WHOA !
AAH!

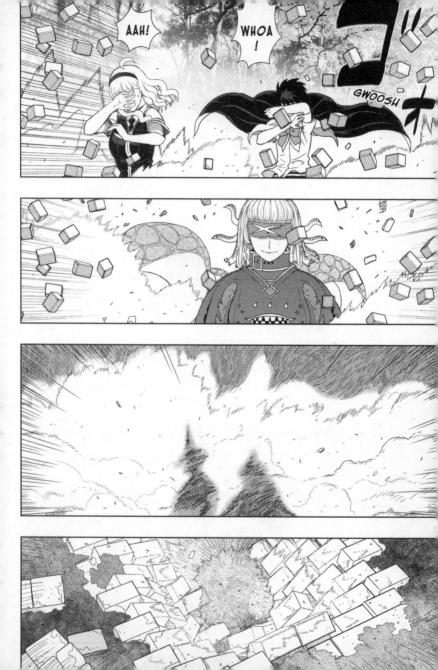

ZHAA
ZHAA
ZHAA
ZHAA

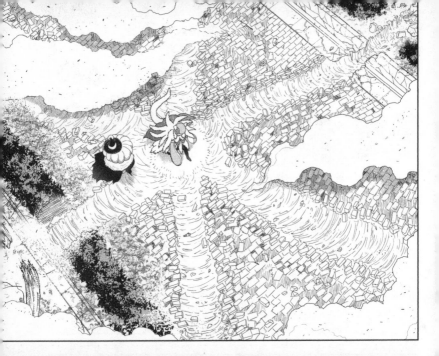

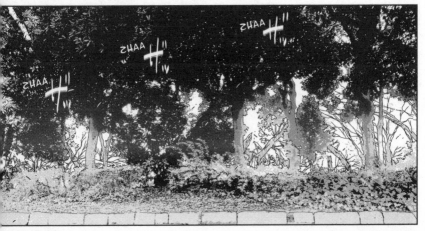

Not a bad body at all. I think I like it.
Heh heh.
This woman is now trapped inside of me... where she will live with me forever.
S-Senpai...
Give her... back...
KASUMI ...!

CHAPTER 32 END

Witchcraft Works

CHAPTER 82.5 Miss Komachi's Delightful Lunch

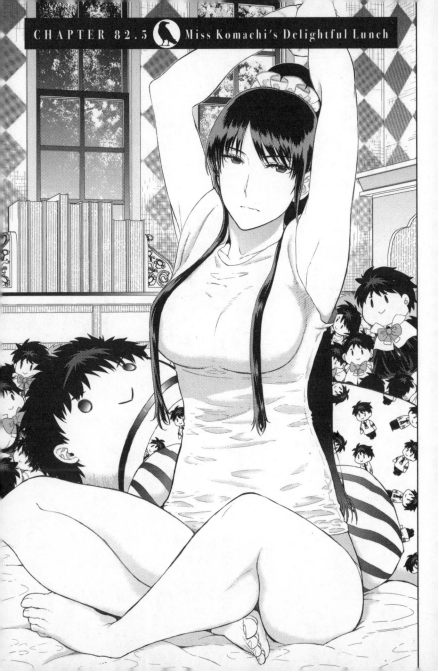

THE STORY UNTIL NOW, ACCORDING TO FURRY-EAR.
IT WAS AN HOUR EARLIER WHEN I, THE GREAT TANPOPO, DAUGHTER OF MISTRESS MEDUSA, THE GRAND TOWER WITCH, NOTICED THAT SOMETHING STRANGE HAD HAPPENED IN THE TOWN.
I LEFT HOME WITH MY MINION (THE TAKAMIYA SISTER) AND MOMMY.
FROM THERE, I MET WITH MY COMRADES AT MISTRESS ME-DUSA'S HOME.
My glasses...
WE DECIDED TO HEAD TO SAFETY, AND WE BRILLIANTLY AVOIDED ANY ENEMIES THANKS TO MY MAGNIFICENT LEADERSHIP AS I MADE EXCELLENT USE OF MY FAMILIARS.
BUT THEN THE TAKAMIYA SISTER SUDDENLY LEFT TOGETHER WITH THE HOODED WITCH ACTING AS OUR GUIDE.
WE'D BEEN LEFT HIGH AND DRY!
...They just left.
But we don't know where to go...
RABBITRABBITRABBIT!
What's that? Enemies are approaching?
There's a park that way, Tanpopo! Let's hide there!
RABBIIIIT

ズ ーーーン
SLUUUUUUUUMP
SIGH
...
What should we do, Sister ...?
AFTER THAT WOMAN BOSSED US AROUND FOR ALL THAT TIME...
SHE DECIDES TO KEEP US IN THE DARK NOW? WHY?!
ザッ
CHFF
Hm? Who the hell are you? If you can move, you must be witches, right?
WE SHOULD BE ASKING YOU THAT!
Tanpopo, I've seen these two before. These two old ladies are janitors at school.
WHO ARE YOU CALLING AN OLD LADY?! I'M CLEARLY A BEAUTI-FUL YOUNG WOMAN!
AAHHH

TROMP TROMP TROMP TROMP TROMP TROMP TROMP
GRAAAAAAH!!
DAMN! OUT OF AMMO!
HEY, YOU OVER THERE! YOU CAN USE MAGIC, CAN'T YOU? DO SOMETHING ABOUT THIS!!
WE'RE OUT OF FIRE-POWER, TOO!!
TSK!
FWOOSH
LET'S GO, GIRLS!
THOKK

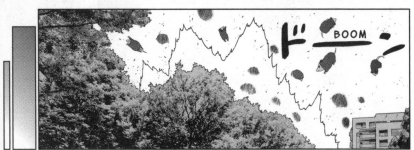

ドーーー
BOOM
Whew. You saved us there. Thanks.
What were you all doing ...?
HEY! ALL OF YOU!

WERE YOU JUST USING MAGIC? I THINK YOU WERE!
WORKSHOP WITCHES SHOULDN'T BE ABLE TO USE ANY RIGHT NOW!
IN OTHER WORDS, YOU MUST BE TOWER WITCHES!
SO WHAT IF WE ARE?!
I HAVE A DUTY TO CAPTURE ANY TOWER WITCHES! THAT'S WHAT!
YOU MIGHT EVEN KNOW MEDUSA'S WHEREABOUTS! IT'S TIME TO TORTURE YOU UNTIL YOU SPIT OUT EVERY-THING YOU KNOW!!
DON'T YOU MOVE AN INCH!!
Let's go Vine!
Yes, Sister!
バ
FLAP
ザ

!
!!
ゴ
DUN
ゴ
DUN
ゴ
DUN
ゴ
DUN
ゴ
DUN
ゴ
DUN
ぱ
KLAP
ん
OH! I KNOW!
!!

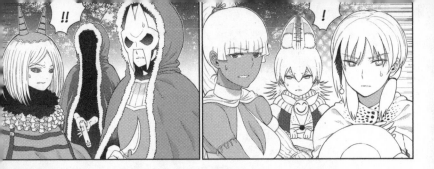

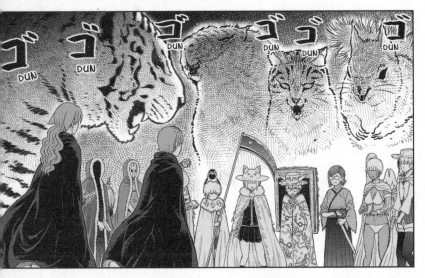

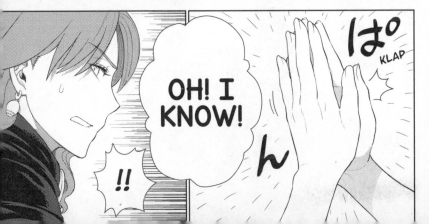

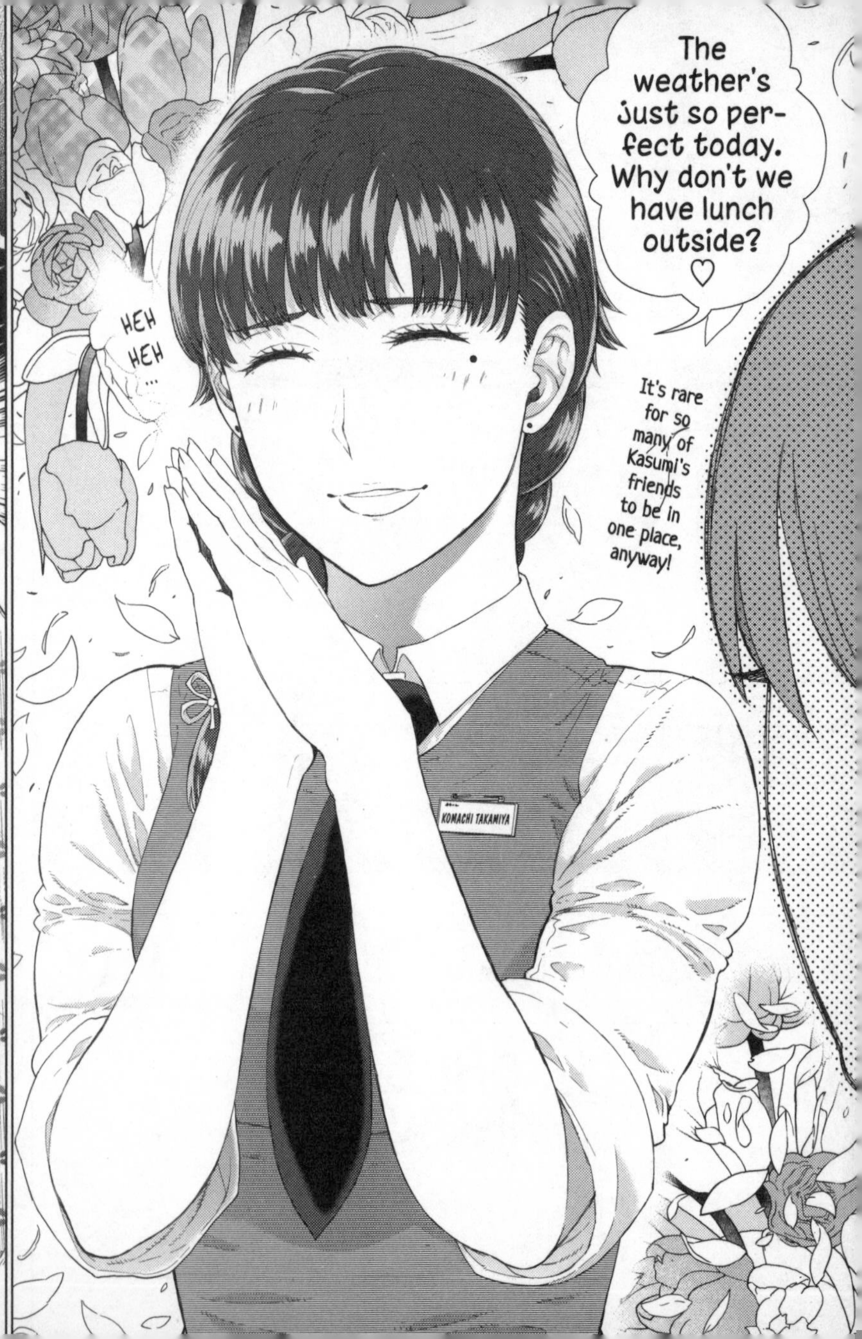
The weather's just so perfect today. Why don't we have lunch outside? ♡
It's rare for so many of Kasumi's friends to be in one place, anyway!
HEH HEH ...
KOMACHI TAKAMIYA

And wouldn't you know it, I made a bunch of sandwiches this morning! ♡

ドーン

BOOM

Tanpopo...

I CAN'T HELP IT!! STOMACHS DON'T LIE!!

...Mommy, I don't think this is the time for...

GROOWWWWLLL

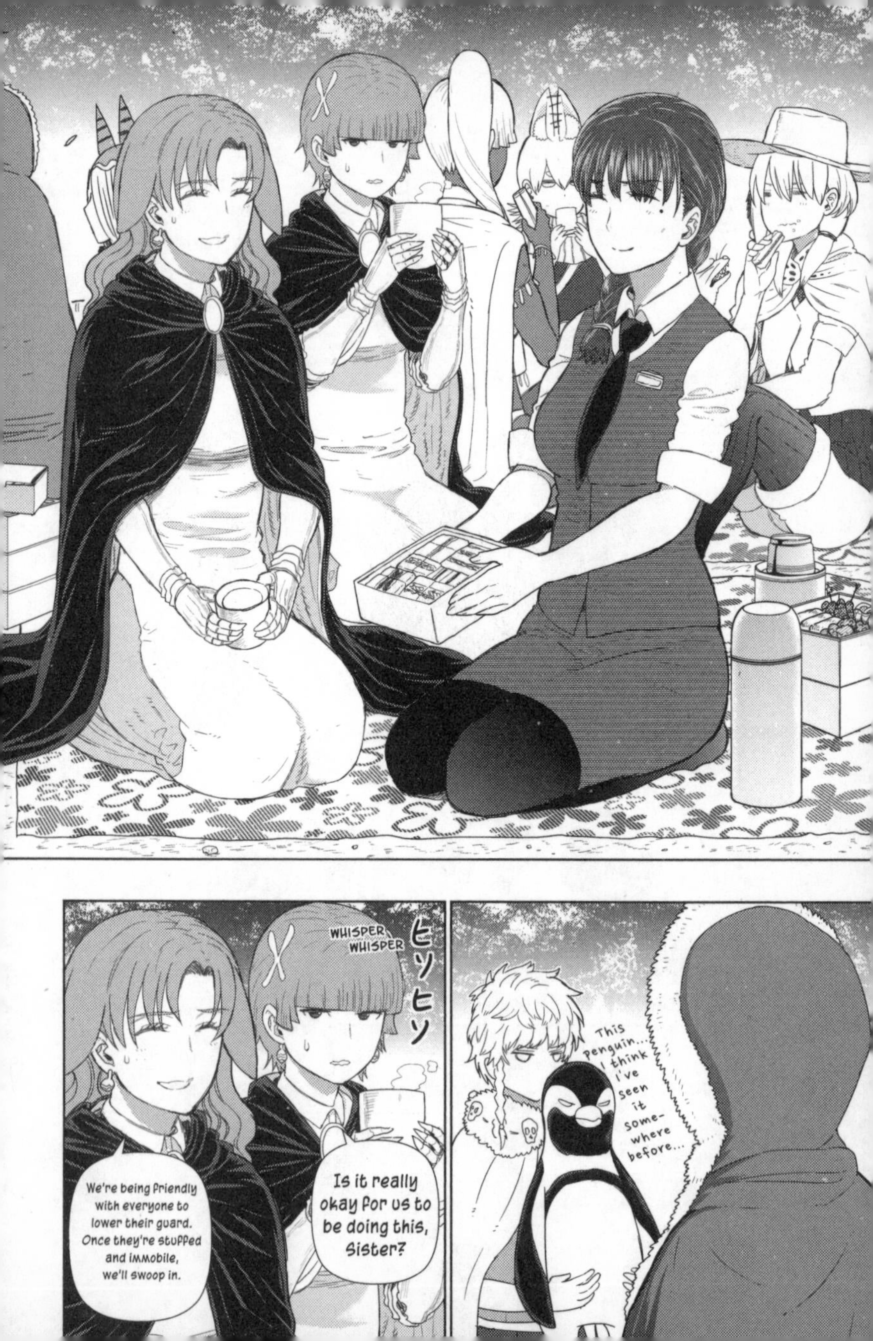
This penguin... I think I've seen it somewhere before...
ヒソヒソ
WHISPER WHISPER
Is it really okay for us to be doing this, Sister?
We're being friendly with everyone to lower their guard. Once they're stuffed and immobile, we'll swoop in.

RABBIT...

NEW YORK SOUL

SWING
ブンブ

AAHN

ズズーン
ZWOOOOOM
?!
Wh-what was that?!
AN EARTH-QUAKE?!
ばっ
BAM
Are you okay, Mommy?!
Yes...
ズキ
THROB

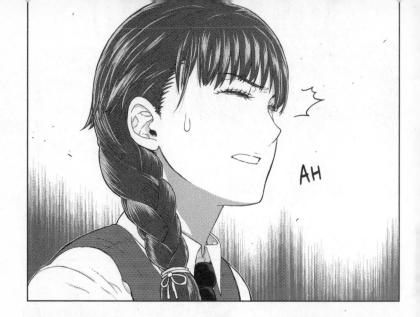

AH
DASH
I need to go! Kasumi, she's ...!
WHERE ARE YOU GOING, MOMMY ?!

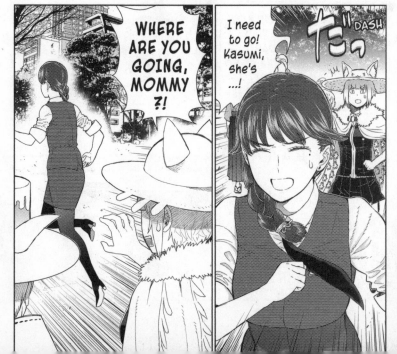

FLAP
LET'S GO, GIRLS! WE'RE PROTECTING MOMMY!
YEEAAH
THD THD THD
SISTER! THEY'VE SPLIT INTO TWO GROUPS!
WHAT DO WE DO?!
...Gah! What cowards...!
GLANCE
GLANCE
Pick up the Pace!
...
Hrmm...!
FOR NOW, WE'LL CAPTURE THE ONES STILL HERE!
GRR
I HOPE YOU'RE READY!
WHAAAA?

Witchcraft Works

CHAPTER 83 Takamiya vs. Alcina: Part 7

Urgh ...
ザ
ZHFF
ザ
ZHFF

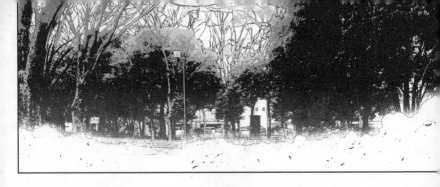

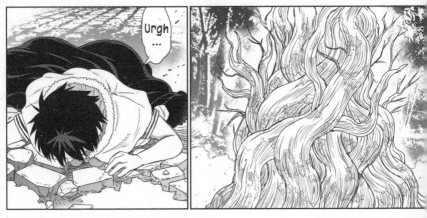

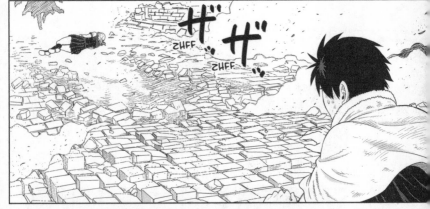

This body isn't bad at all.

I think I'll make you a part of it as well.

Ngh...

GRRT

Kasumi.

KEEP YOUR HANDS OFF OF KASUMI !!
だっ
DASH
HMPH.
だん
BWAM
ががが
GRAK
GRAK
GRAK
GRAK
THWOK
ゴパ
WAAH !
ZZSHHH
ザザッ

You stay there and be a good boy, Takamiya.
All right... Now that there's no one left to get in my way, time to enjoy some dessert...
BOOM
GRAK
GRAK
GRAK

GUH

ガ"

GRAK

...!
BAM
You must have some pretty ridiculous strength to get out of a binding spell.
And now you want to use it to choke me out, eh?
I know you can't use magic right now, but still. How pathetic.
Get-ting out of this is—

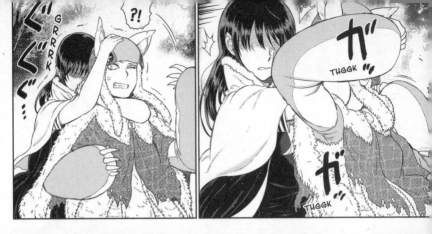

ガ
THGGK
ガ
THGGK
?!
ぐぐぐ…
GRRRK
Shit! Let go!
ドカ
THWAK
バカ
WHAKK
You really are too strong for your own good!!
SNICKER
SNICKER
Hey! What's going on here?! Is it magic that's making her arms so bizarrely powerful?! Workshop witches shouldn't be able to use magic, right?!
Oh, no. That really is just sheer, brute strength.

Have you forgotten? She serves the White Princess.

Ah, if only you'd stayed a dog. Then you wouldn't have ended up in such a sorry state...

...!

ぐ ぐ ぐ GRRRK

ド ド THUD

HAA
HAA
HAA
TOTTER
HAA
HAA
ZHFF
You did an impressive job there, but you're all scraped up now. Are you really going to try to challenge me in such condition?
You've taken all of the damage that should've gone to Takamiya as well, right?
HAA
HAA

...That doesn't concern you.

Urgh...

BAM

?!

Uh oh. Looks like Takamiya's about to wake up.

USE THIS!
ぼっ
SWOOP
ぱし
CATCH
...
Thanks...
ごしごし
SCRUB
SCRUB
HAA HAA HAA
HAAAAAH!

Ngh... Ka...gari...

Are you okay, Takamiya?

BAM
SHIT!
JUMP
I let my guard down!
ピタッ
HALT
!!

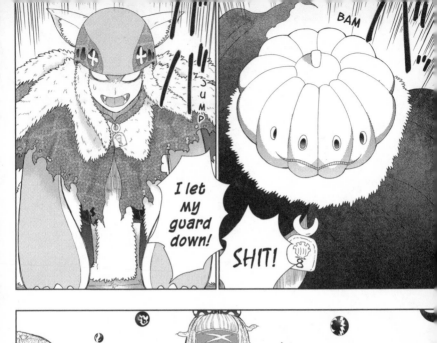

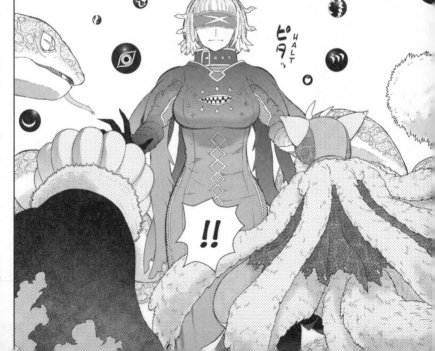

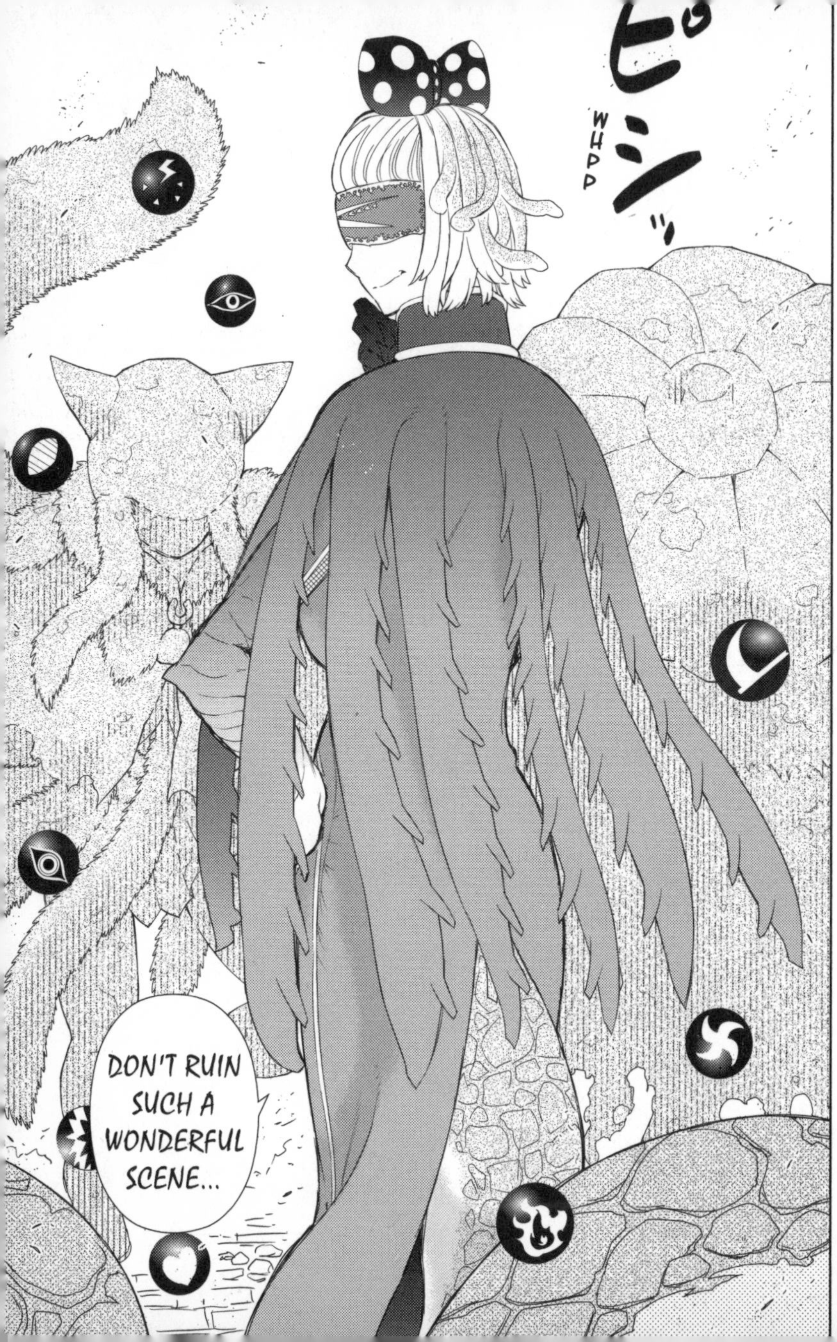
ピシッ
WHPP
DON'T RUIN SUCH A WONDERFUL SCENE...

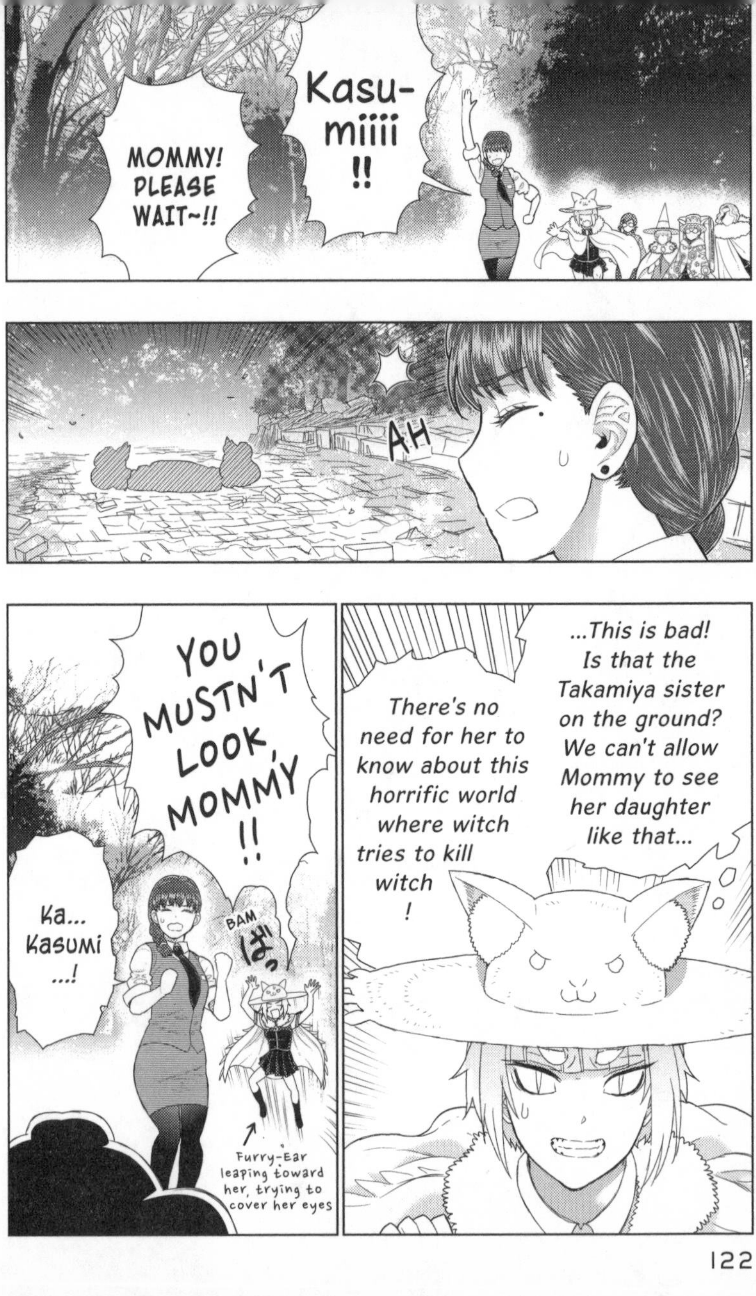
Kasu-miiii !!
MOMMY! PLEASE WAIT~!!
AH
...This is bad! Is that the Takamiya sister on the ground? We can't allow Mommy to see her daughter like that...
There's no need for her to know about this horrific world where witch tries to kill witch !
YOU MUSTN'T LOOK, MOMMY !!
BAM ぱっ
Ka... Kasumi ...!
Furry-Ear leaping toward her, trying to cover her eyes

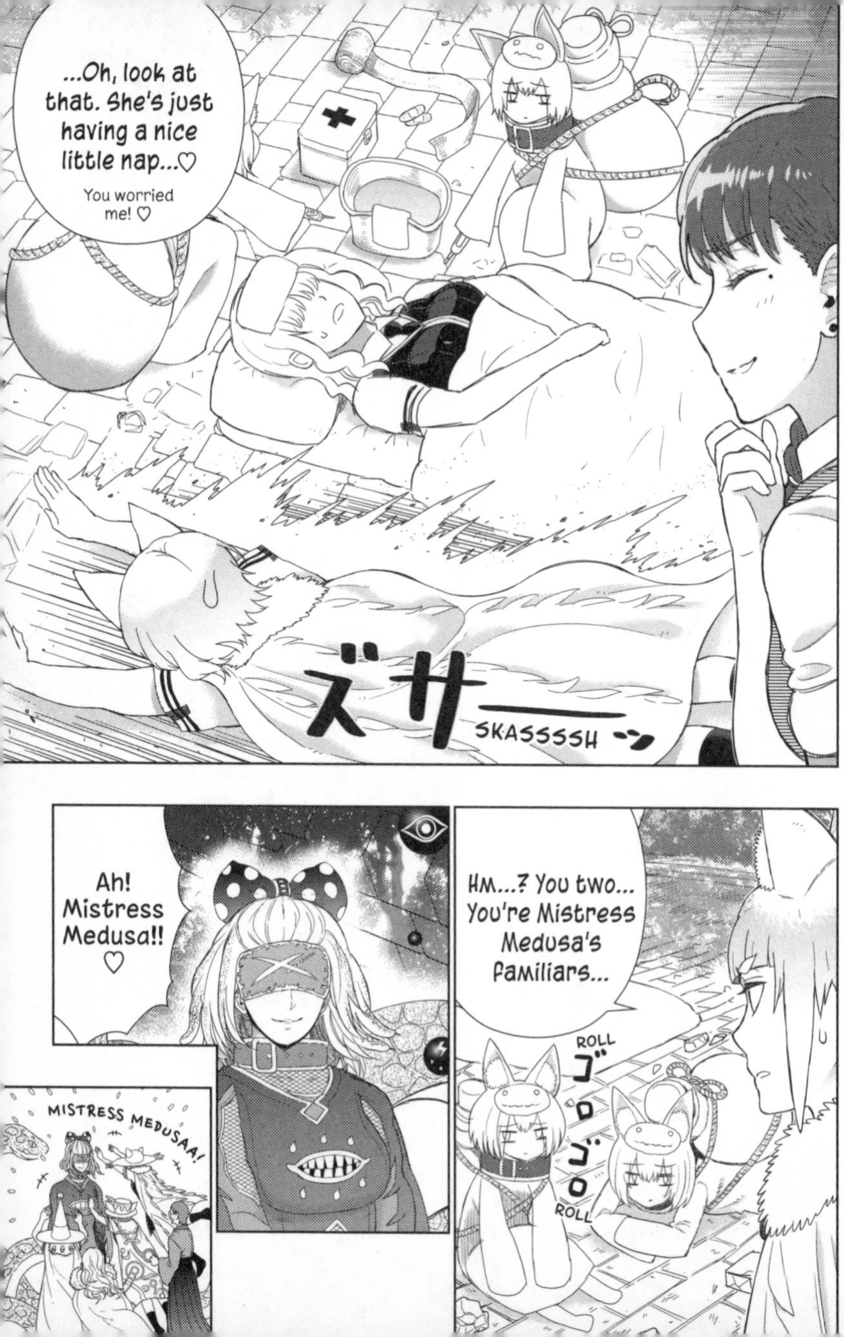
...Oh, look at that. She's just having a nice little nap...♡
You worried me! ♡
ズサー
SKASSSSH
Hm...? You two... You're Mistress Medusa's familiars...
ROLL
ゴロゴロ
ROLL
Ah! Mistress Medusa!! ♡
MISTRESS MEDUSAA!

...Now, then. You're willing to come with me, Takamiya?
...You want to take me to Alcina, don't you?
As much as it galls me to do as the Winter Storm says...
well, she allowed me to hold my daughters with my very own hands, so I won't complain...
By the way... should you really have petrified those two...?
They'll return to normal on their own in no time. As members of Hydra Head, they're reasonably capable witches.

...I guess you were after me, too, now that I think about it...
Of course... And I'll do what needs to be done when the time comes.
ちらっ
GLANCE
Kagari's acting like she's fine, but... she must've taken a lot of damage already...

All right. Please take me to Alcina.

Witchcraft Works

All right. Please take me to Alcina.

Very well. Then follow me, Takamiya.

CHAPTER 84 Takamiya vs. Alcina: Part 8

HUH?! HERE?!

It's right this way. Ready to go?

...L-Like... right here? Is this a joke?
You think I would make a joke?
...
Takamiya... this could be a trap. This place is clearly suspicious.
BAM
E- EXCUSE ME...!
WAIT, TAKAMIYA?!
Come on, everyone. Let's go.

Welcome.

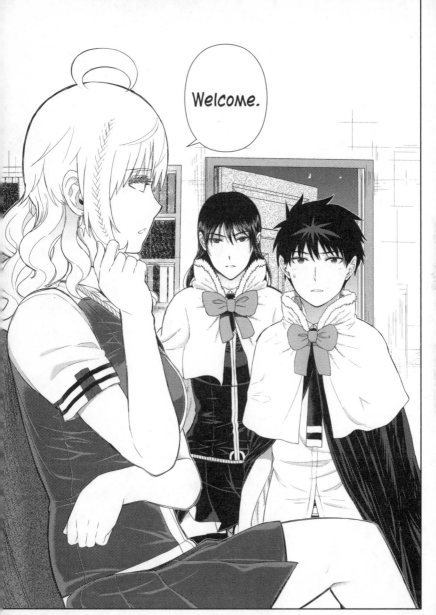

キッ
GRR
だっ
DASH
ズイ
SWOOP
Calm down, Ayaka.
Chair-wo-man!
Hello, Taka-miya.
Uncivi-lized as always, I see.
Not that I dislike that about you.
It's been a while, Hono-ka.
ぬっ
LOOM
!!
Okay, that's enough. Don't you work her up too, Shiori.
Honestly, you guys...
グイ
SHOVE
GEH HEH HEH
GRRR

...Only children let themselves get carried away by their emotions, you know. You need to be more rational when...
HAAH
Kazane!!
KOMACHI?!
ガッ
GRAB
Oh, I wanted to see you so badly, Kazane! I was so scared, the town's acting all funny~!
Mom...
...Honoka? Has Komachi been moving around normally this entire time?
What? Yes, she has. Why do you ask...?

...Even so, it's strange for Komachi to be here in this world of witches. I feel a slight amount of mana coming from her, too. I may need to look into this...
I'd like our injured to recuperate.
We added a sickroom just past that door.
HUP TWO HUP TWO
Why are you here, Chair-woman?
CHATTER
Well, the situation has gotten compli-cated...
And hey, Komachi, can you not be so clingy...?
CHATTER
...
BAM
HEY! ALL OF YOU! I'M THE ONE IN CHARGE HERE! DO YOU UNDERSTAND THE SITUATION YOU'RE IN RIGHT NOW?!

Yes, I know.

KIORA!

THOK THOK THOK THOK THOK THOK
ガ ガ ガ ガ ガ ガ

カ
ニ
シ
ャ

GASHANG

TAKA-MIYA!
Oh ho, it seems the bothersome part is about to begin. I'll be taking my leave now.
Sure. Good work out there, Medusa.
ガチャ
GACHIK
CONTRACT
That brings an end to our contract.
ペラ
FLAP
CONTRACT
ピシッ
PSSHT
This makes us enemies once more.
Yes. I'll make you into a nice piece of furniture the next time we meet.
ザッ
ZHFF
パラパラ
CRUMBLE CRUMBLE

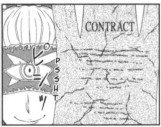

The exit's over there.
By the way, Medusa... Leave the Workshop witches you're carrying here with you.
Why are you carrying Workshop witches to begin with?
Excuse me? These girls are my daughters.
...Daughters? Wait, you were all Tower witches ?!
HOLD ON A SECOND !!
They're already past the gate. They left.
Argh, geez. This town is just full of problems. I'm looking into this later, Kazane.
Ack ...
...Okay. Let's get down to business.
Kiora! Set the stage!
Very well.
FLASH

FLAP

TH—
THIS IS ...!
BOOM
DEFENDANT HONOKA TAKAMIYA! YOUR TRIAL HEREBY BEGINS!
TRIAL ?! OVER WHAT ?!
You can't talk your way out of this one. We already know that you're a spy connected to our enemies.
What? No, I'm not trying to talk my way out of anything... I don't know what you're talking about. Connected to your enemies? W-Well, Tower witches are staying at my home... is that it?!
Even so, they might be a little odd, but they're good people! They're friends with my sister Kasumi, too...
It's nothing that trivial.
If you're going to keep on feigning ignorance, then fine.
I'll just try you in my own way.
...I've already heard enough of your defense. There's no point in wasting any more time.
I'll deliver my judge-ment.
WHAT?! THAT WAS FAST!

THE COURT'S DECISION IS AS FOLLOWS! WE FIND DEFENDANT HONOKA TAKAMIYA GUILTY! HE WILL BE TORTURED UNTIL HE GIVES US INFORMATION ABOUT OUR ENEMIES, AND FOLLOW-ING THAT, I EXERCISE MY POWERS AS PARISH AUDITOR TO SEND YOU TO ULTIMA THULE!
YOU WILL SERVE THIS PUNISHMENT FOR ETERNITY! WE WILL BE RESPONSIBLE FOR MANAGING AND SEALING AWAY YOUR SOUL AS WELL!
THIS DECISION CONCLUDES THE MATTER! COURT IS HEREBY ADJOURNED!
AM
BA
H... H-H-HOLD ...
HOLD ON JUST A SECOND!
I HAVEN'T DONE ANY-THING WRONG!
THAT'S RIGHT! I OBJECT! THIS TRIAL IS WAY TOO ONE-SIDED!

We have hard evidence that he is a traitor.
Of course it's one-sided. I only did this as a matter of process. The decision was set from the start.
I don't know what kind of proof you might have, but I'm absolutely sure that Takamiya is innocent.
You're going to let us make our counter-argument.
Ka-gari ...
You are a Work-shop witch with respect for law and order, are you not?
YEAH! WHAT MY DAUGHTER SAID!
...
...How amusing. Fine, I'd like to see you try.
SNAP
パチン
ZZT
ZZT

Atori.
ぬっ
BLOOP
Oh. So you had a witch hiding there.
You did notice her, right, Kiora?
I let her be. She's harmless.
And?
What is this little furry-eared witch of yours going to present to disprove my claim...?
コク
NOD
ドサッ
SHWUMP
OBSERVATION DIARY.

These are notes that record a year's worth of Takamiya's actions!
BOOM
If you need more, we'll bring them from home!
Every last thing that Takamiya does during the day is recorded in here!
This is my magnum opus!
Month O Year XX
7:06 Wake up Earlier than usual
7:08 Toilet Healthy
7:10 Brush teeth No missed spots
7:17 Little sister Wake-up call
7:15 Eat Lots of rice
7:35 Change Swap clothes
7:48 Go to school Princess
7:59 Bus Elderly
8:28 School Locker
8:45 Class Academics
9:32 Little Sister Free time
10:33 Toilet No suspicious
12:10 Food Eating in the
13:10 Class Nap
do homework together
Cheese-stuffed hamburger steak
bath salts
make penguin statue
with Princess
good
Hey, wait a sec... I knew you were living in my ceiling, Atori, but is this what you were really up to?
It's so detailed...
So what? You think that counts as proof?
We have more than journals.
We even have videos and photos.
USB

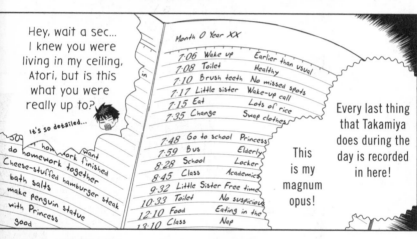

But I know you'd never believe my records, no matter how many I present! But that's where I have you. I'm not the only one keeping a close eye on Takamiya.
His little sister does, too, and your own underlings are as well!!
I'D LIKE TO CALL A WITNESS TO THE STAND!
So everyone just knows that those two are tailing him...?
...Kiora. Can you summon the two tattooed sisters?
Yes. I can summon those two at any time.
ズズズ
ZZZM
ACK!
ドドド
THWUMP
OWWW!
UGH! WHAT DO YOU WANT?!

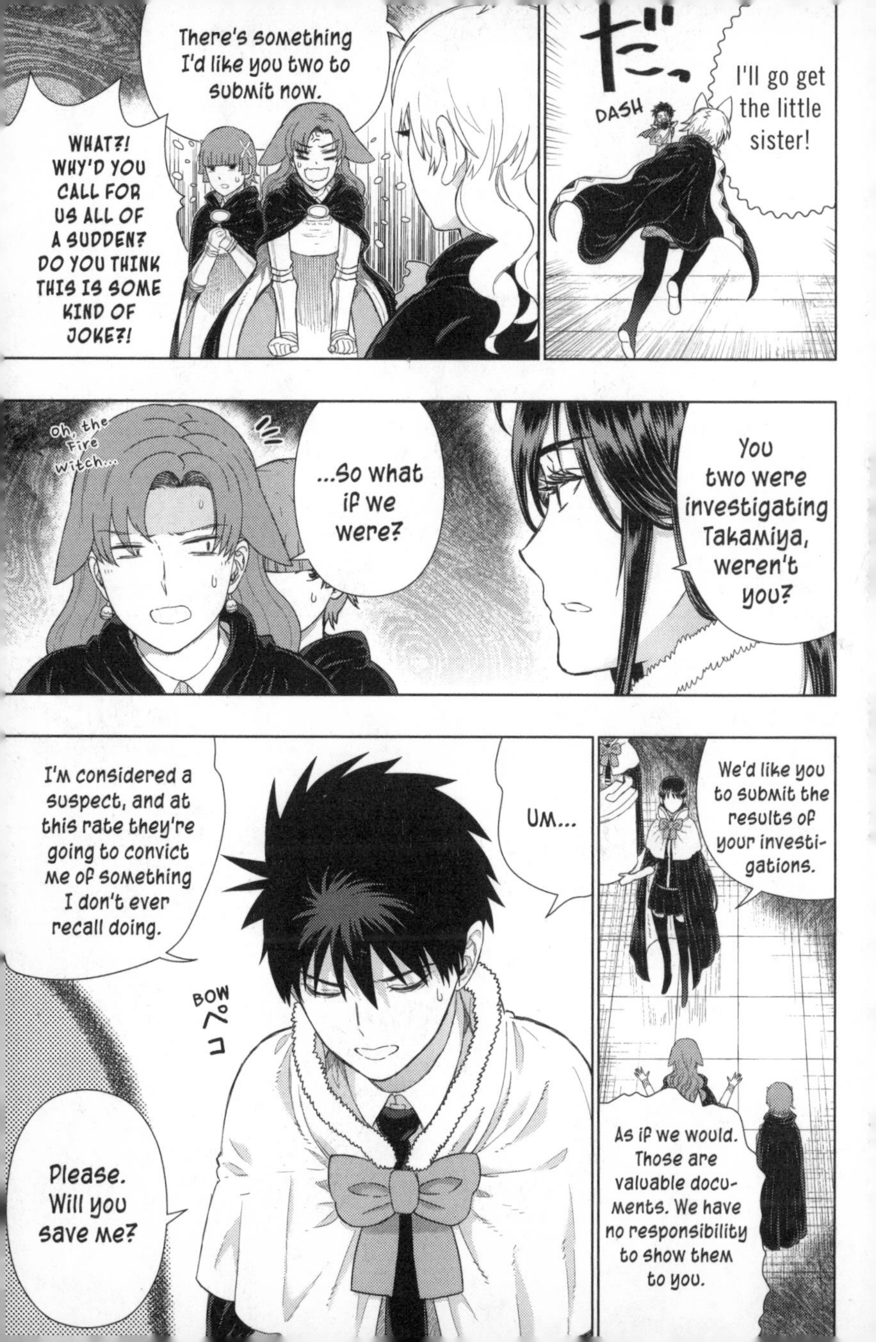
だっ
DASH
I'll go get the little sister!
There's something I'd like you two to submit now.
WHAT?! WHY'D YOU CALL FOR US ALL OF A SUDDEN? DO YOU THINK THIS IS SOME KIND OF JOKE?!
You two were investigating Takamiya, weren't you?
...So what if we were?
Oh, the Fire Witch...
We'd like you to submit the results of your investi-gations.
As if we would. Those are valuable docu-ments. We have no responsibility to show them to you.
Um...
I'm considered a suspect, and at this rate they're going to convict me of something I don't ever recall doing.
BOW
ペコ
Please. Will you save me?

W-Well... Just this... one time... okay?
HUH?
BDUM
ドキ
バ
BAM
Thank you so much!
がしっ
GRASP
I got the little sister!
HONOKA'S IN TROUBLE?! THIS IS NO TIME TO BE SLEEPING!!
たたた
THP THP THP
JUST WAIT! I'LL PROVE TAKAMIYA'S INNOCENCE!

CHAPTER 84 END

Witchcraft Works

7:12. WAKE UP. NO IRREGU-LARITIES.
LITTLE SISTER HAD SNUCK INTO HIS BED THE DAY BEFORE. AFTER NOTICING, HE CARRIED HER ON HIS BACK TO HER ROOM.
A REGULAR OCCUR-RENCE FOR HIM.
MY LITTLE POTATO
GREETED THE PRINCESS IN THE HALLWAY.
WHOOPS, THIS PART ISN'T RELATED.
7:45. BREAKFAST. GETS A SECOND HELPING OF RICE. SAME AS ALWAYS.
CHOMP
CHOMP
MUNCH
MUNCH
INCIDENTALLY, THIS IS WHEN LITTLE SISTER PICKS A FIGHT WITH THE PRIN-CESS, LEADING TO A HOLE BEING OPENED IN THE CEILING.
UGH. WHO DO THEY THINK IS ALWAYS REPAIRING THE DAMAGE TO THIS HOUSE?
MRRGH

Following this, changed into the uniform prepared the previous night by the Princess and left for school—
How long do you plan on going, exactly?
It's not like I'm interested in knowing what he does on an average day.
イライラ UUUGH
トン TAP
トン TAP
CHAPTER 85 Takamiya vs. Alcina: Part 9

H-HOLD ON! WAIT! WHY ARE YOU SURVEYING EVERY LITTLE THING THAT HONOKA DOES?!
'Cuz that's my job!
Your job? Who would ask you to...?
GLANCE
ちらっ
Oh. It'd have to be the Princess, of course.
Nampus
TAKAMIYA OBSERVATION DIARY
Huh? That note-book...
I've seen it before...

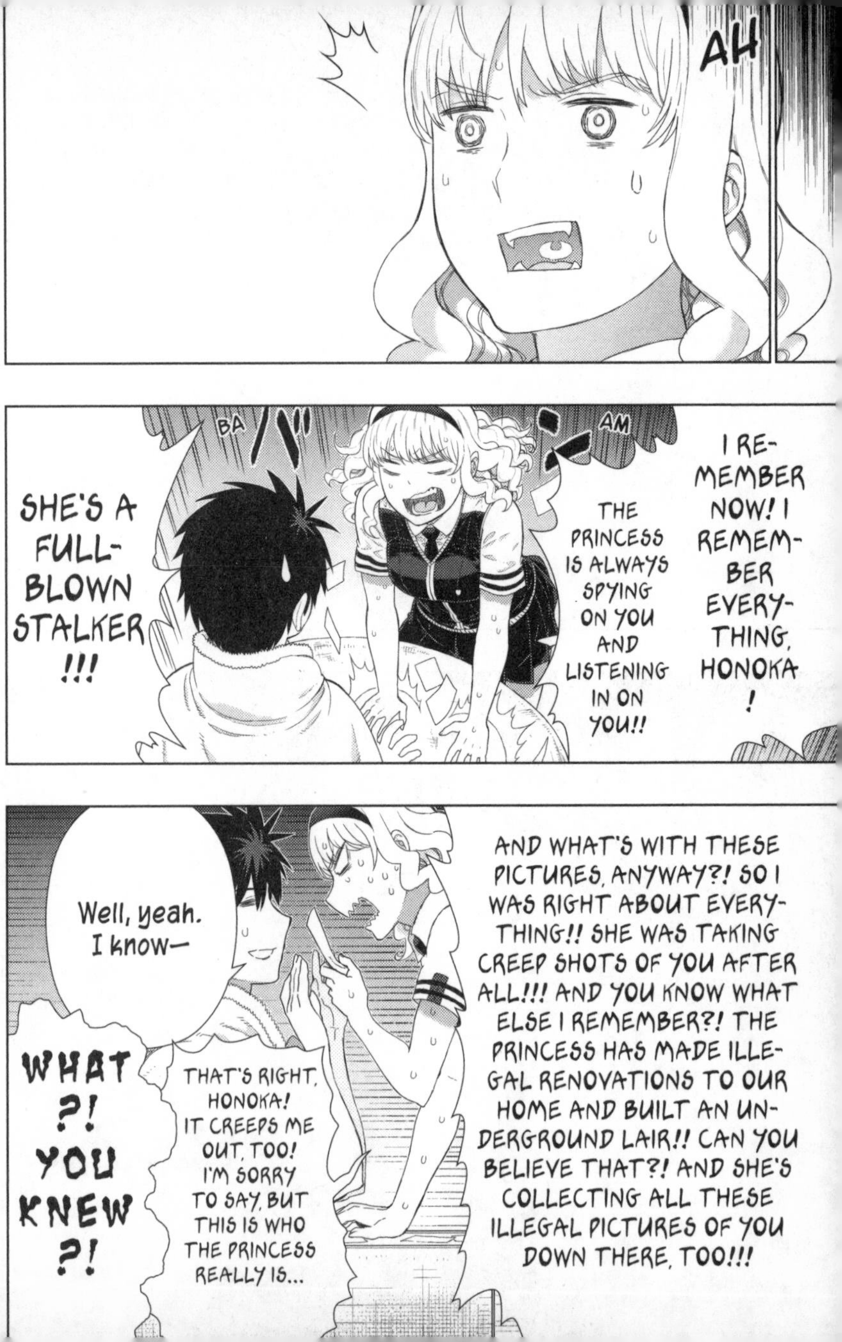
AH
I RE-MEMBER NOW! I REMEM-BER EVERY-THING, HONOKA!
AM
BA
THE PRINCESS IS ALWAYS SPYING ON YOU AND LISTENING IN ON YOU!!
SHE'S A FULL-BLOWN STALKER!!!
AND WHAT'S WITH THESE PICTURES, ANYWAY?! SO I WAS RIGHT ABOUT EVERY-THING!! SHE WAS TAKING CREEP SHOTS OF YOU AFTER ALL!!! AND YOU KNOW WHAT ELSE I REMEMBER?! THE PRINCESS HAS MADE ILLE-GAL RENOVATIONS TO OUR HOME AND BUILT AN UN-DERGROUND LAIR!! CAN YOU BELIEVE THAT?! AND SHE'S COLLECTING ALL THESE ILLEGAL PICTURES OF YOU DOWN THERE, TOO!!!
THAT'S RIGHT, HONOKA! IT CREEPS ME OUT, TOO! I'M SORRY TO SAY, BUT THIS IS WHO THE PRINCESS REALLY IS...
Well, yeah. I know—
WHAT?! YOU KNEW?!

Kagari's doing it to protect me, right?

HA HA

I admit I didn't know Atori had gone that far, though.

?!

...

NO, HONOKA! THAT'S NOT HOW YOU SHOULD REACT!! IS EVERYTHING OKAY WITH YOU?! YOU'RE ACTING WEIRD!
HAS THE PRINCESS BRAINWASHED YOU? OH, THAT'S IT! THAT HAS TO BE IT! WAKE UP, HONOKA!!
BAM
What? Brain-washed?
If anything, I don't appre-ciate the way you always talk about Kagari like she's some kind of criminal.
HUH? WHAT?! AM I THE WEIRD ONE HERE?!
SLUMP
Little sister has suddenly dropped out from the team!
So, Alcina?
Why do you suspect him of anything in the first place?
He's colluding with our enemies.
Collud-ing?
...

HE'S NEVER DONE ANYTHING LIKE THAT IN THE TIME SINCE I STARTED MONITORING HIM, AT LEAST!
BA
HERE'S THE PROOF !!
BOOM
THAT'S A LOT OF PROOF !!
I-I HAVE SOME, TOO !!
SST
DIARY
She's back in action!
IT'S NOT ALL ABOUT QUANTITY, OKAY ?!
Look at all the proof we've got!
And what proof do you have that he's guilty ?!
FWOOM

This.
FWT
...
TH-
THAT'S
...!

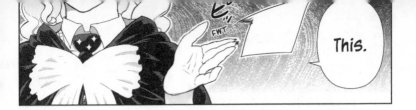

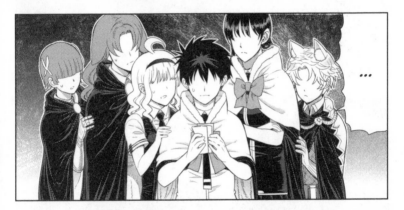

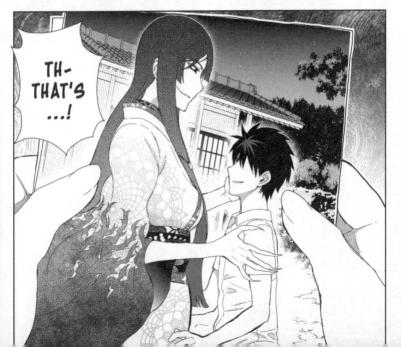

HOLD ON A SECOND! THAT ISN'T ME!
UM, OKAY, IT MIGHT LOOK LIKE ME! BUT—
That's impossible. I've used magic to confirm that it's not a fake there. The test came back saying that the man in the picture is Honoka Takamiya.
When did it happen?
Some time last week.
So all we need is an alibi for the week, then?
Last week... Wait, that's when we went out without the Princess!
You spent a whole day with me!
That day, you went with us...
And on this day we trained in the yard!
And you held hands with the Princess this day!
WHAT?! I NEVER HEARD ABOUT THAT!!

LOOK! THERE'S PLENTY OF EVIDENCE TO BACK US UP!
WHAT DO YOU SAY TO THAT?!
...
In that case, there's a contra-diction here.
Where'd you get that evidence from, any-way?
My underlings... Isn't that right, Kiora?
...Yes.
...More importantly, Alcina, two members of Hydra Head are requesting entry.
HM? ...Fine. Let them in.

BAM
Medusa! Where are you ?!
If it's Medusa you're looking for, she already left.
I expected you to make yourselves at least a little useful, but—
ホソ
WHISPER
You really are all bark and no bite.
What ?! What did you just...
Shut up! I just let my guard down, that's all!!

You heard me. I said I can't stand having to be right next to a noisy, whimpering dog like you.

...Who are you?

...

AYAKA! DON'T LET HER FOOL YOU! SHE'S A FAKE! RESTRAIN HER AT ONCE!!

Whoa now.

SCHK
スチッ

?!

BAM

!

Natsume, what are you doing ...?
KIO-RA!
She should have been restrained by the Workshop's tree, right?
Hm... That's strange. That's unmistakably Natsume Mikage... but she was unmistakably a member of Hydra Head until just now... and Natsume Mikage continues to be restrained... Hmm.

Wait, the Natsume who attacked you in the past, Shiori ...?
Yes, that's her! She's one of that woman's agents.
...! So this is all her doing.
ALCINA! THAT WOMAN'S VERY EXISTENCE IS PROOF OF TAKAMIYA'S INNOCENCE!
STILL!
That said, it doesn't change the fact that you hid the facts from us.
Kiora! Restrain her for now!
Well, Alcina... I've been trying to do just that for a while.
She's resisting my magic... I don't understand.

What a splendid witch you are, with your ability to transmute your very self. An incantation? Magic that shaves away life itself...?
And it's been centuries since I've last encountered it...
You possess the mirrored orb with the ability to resist my dimensional magic, do you not?
How keen of you.
...How do you have...
Kiora! Seal this classroom... no, this entire school! Burrows! Tattooed witches! Capture her!

She has already activated it.

It is too late.

Purification Field.

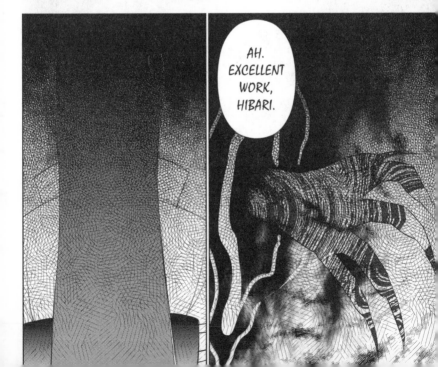

AH. EXCELLENT WORK, HIBARI.

MY DEAR HONOKA. HOW LONG IT'S BEEN SINCE WE LAST MET.
?!

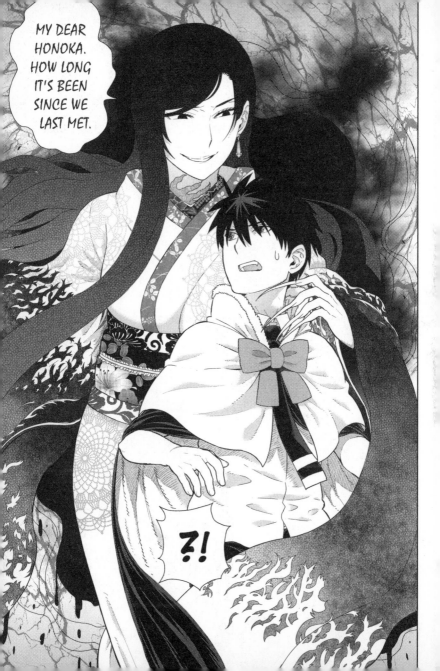

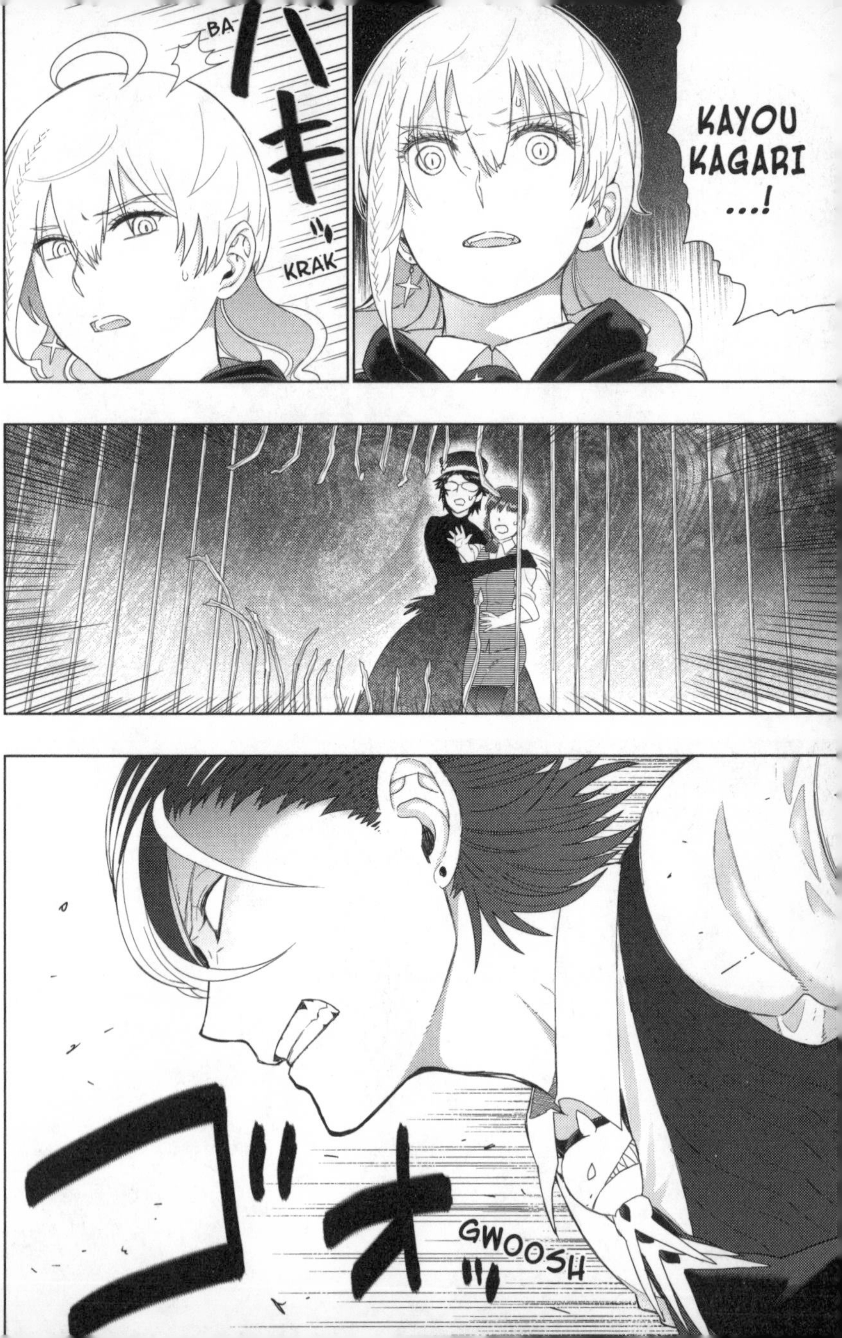
KAYOU
KAGARI
...!
BA
ハキッ
KRAK
ゴオッ
GWOOSH

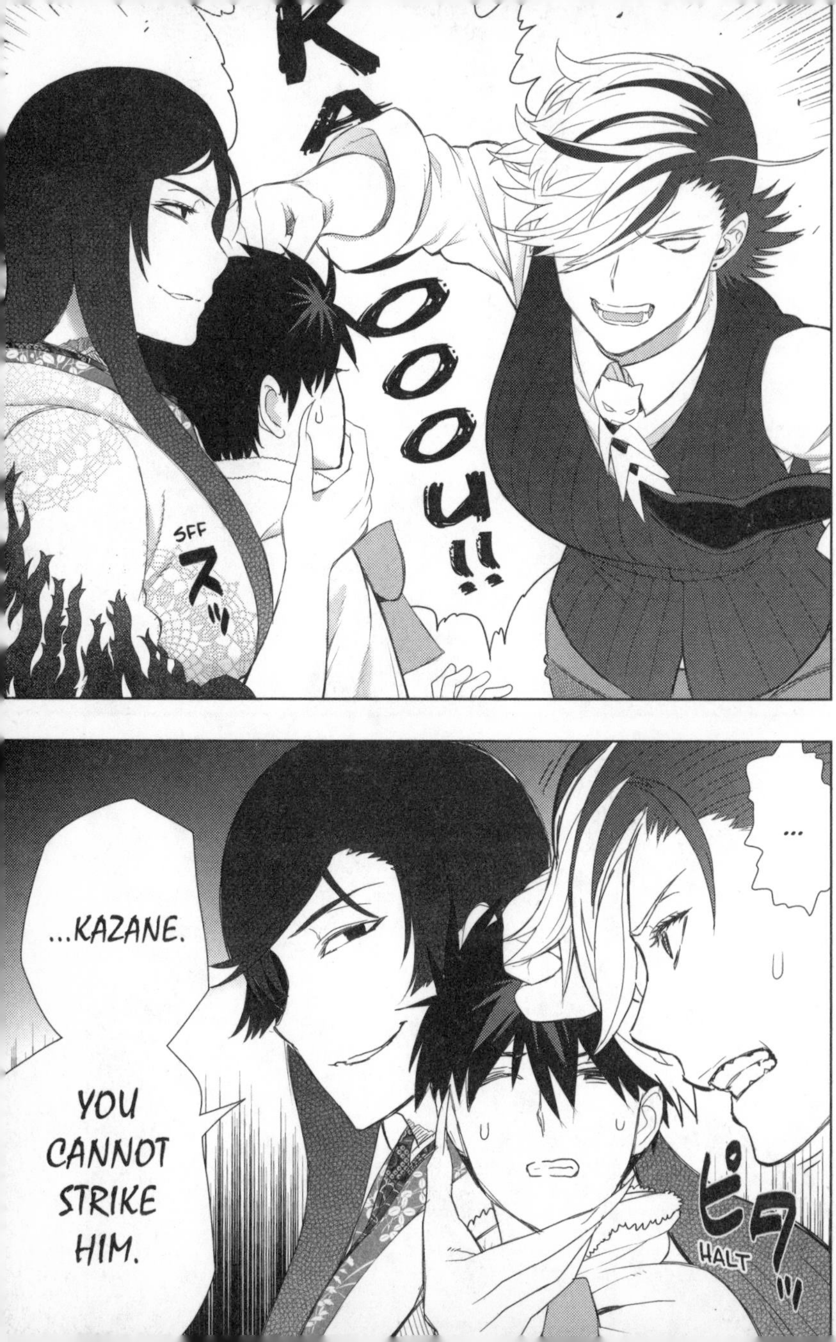
KAOOOU!!
SFF
スッ
...
...KAZANE.
YOU CANNOT STRIKE HIM.
ピクッ
HALT

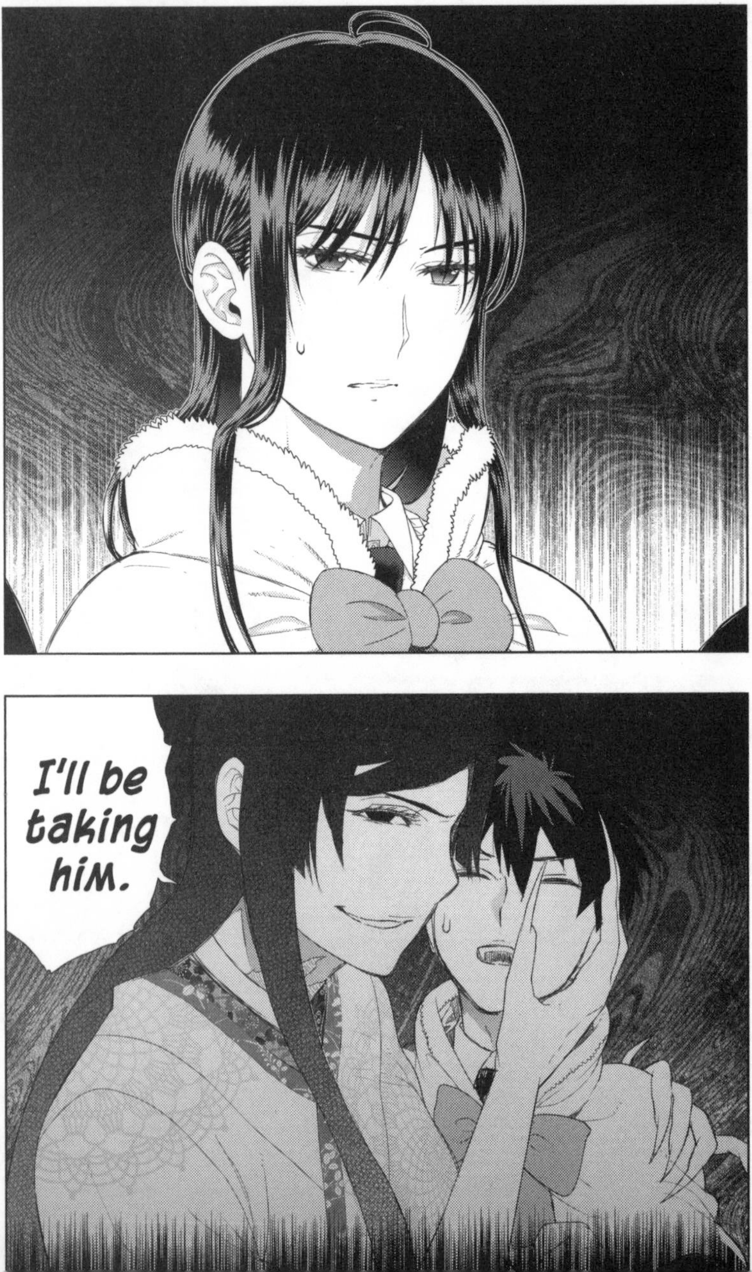
I'll be taking him.

WITCHCRAFT WORKS 14 END

Witchcraft Works

NEW YORK SOUL

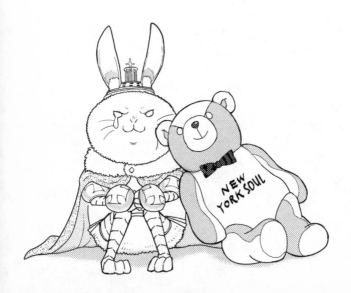

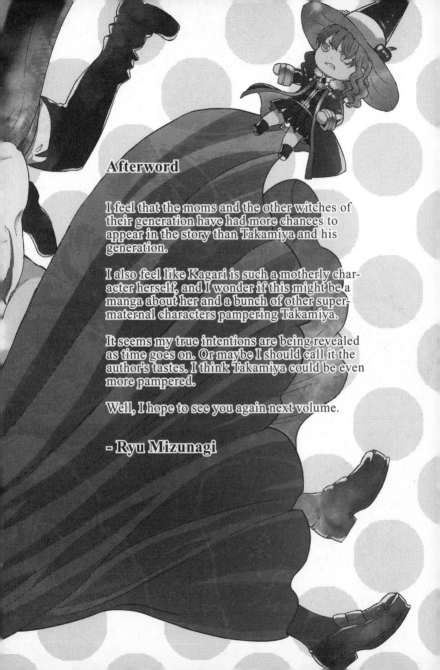

Afterword

I feel that the moms and the other witches of their generation have had more chances to appear in the story than Takamiya and his generation.

I also feel like Kagari is such a motherly character herself, and I wonder if this might be a manga about her and a bunch of other super-maternal characters pampering Takamiya.

It seems my true intentions are being revealed as time goes on. Or maybe I should call it the author's tastes. I think Takamiya could be even more pampered.

Well, I hope to see you again next volume.

- Ryu Mizunagi

Witchcraft Works

WITCHCRAFT WORKS 14

TAKAMIYA'S DAILY LIFE

THESE ARE ALL NOTES RECORDING HIS ACTIONS!
I'VE GOT PHOTOS AND VIDEOS, TOO! WANNA SEE ?!
AND THESE ARE VIDEOS CAPTURING EVERYTHING HE DID!
IF YOU WANT PHOTOS, I'LL GIVE YOU THOSE AS WELL!
I'VE GOT SOME-THING, TOO!
MY DIARY ABOUT HONOKA !!!
I see he doesn't have any privacy... I feel a little bad for him...
And there's the girl who built a museum about him...

Witchcraft Works

This page is a collection of behind-the-scenes character and story elements that probably won't affect or appear in the main story, as well as comments by the author. If you finish reading the story and think, "I want to know more!" then we hope you enjoy the information here.

Chapter 79

Takamiya and Kagari head to the holy ground.

• The Furry-Ear Gang
Kazarin has taken a liking to Takamiya's penguin familiar, often taking it with her and caring for it. They've even started sleeping in the same bed as of late.

• Takamiya and Kagari
The two encounter the fake Natsume while heading toward the holy ground. Kagari quietly grows angry over the fact that she imitated Takamiya.

Chapter 80

A side story from Kasumi's POV.

• Medusa
Medusa has a kind side to her, making food and leaving it for her daughters before setting off early in the morning for her work. Medusa is often away, which means her daughters tend to do the housework.

    Kazarin generally handles cooking. It seems she learned from Komachi when freeloading at the Takamiya home. Cleaning and laundry is handled by Kanna. Mei sometimes helps them when she feels like it, but she usually doesn't do anything. Kotetsu's always busy practicing sword swings and doesn't help out around the house at all.

Tanpopo handled the cooking back when she was around. Her cooking didn't seem to be very popular within the Furry-Ear Gang, though, as it always turned out like cat food.

• Rinon Otometachibana
Comes to save Kasumi and the others on the Chairwoman's orders. She does hold suspicions about Komachi, though, as she's able to move about in the magic-affected town...

• Tanpopo and Mei
Tanpopo maps the area by using a massive number of her mini rabbit soldiers. Mei passes through walls so that they can avoid encountering enemies. They might have turned out to be tough enemies for Takamiya and the rest if only they could get it together.

Chapter 81

Takamiya and Kagari head to the holy ground, Part II.

• Takamiya and Kagari
The two encounter Alcina's underling witches as they head toward the holy ground. Medusa also joins them, having made a deal with Alcina.

• Hydra Head
Witches who have strayed from the path of humanity in search of even greater power. It seems that a witch who once worked with Weekend was with them, too.

Chapter 82

Vs. Hydra Head.

• Medusa
It's discovered that Medusa was the one to stop time in town. She has joined Alcina's side in exchange for her arms being freed.

• Burrowsdate
A witch with a Semicraft that allows her to inherit the powers of any witch she eats. Hydra Head is the name given to the witches who created Semicrafts, imitations of Witchcraft magic. Searching for the ultimate magic,

they created these in order to mass produce Witchcraft, which is unique. Semicraft is difficult for a flesh-and-blood witch to use due to its many impurities, leading to the appearance of witches who had variously thrown away their physical bodies or gained more powerful ones by merging with beasts, etc.

The oldest Semicraft is a Semi-Firecraft, but its power was so unstable and hard to handle that it was split into nine pieces and inherited by nine witches. The name Hydra Head came to be when these witches were compared to the heads of a hydra.

Chapter 82.5

What happened on the Furry-Ear Gang's side.

• The Furry-Ear Gang
They meet with the tattooed witches, the Star Team witches, and Weekend's underlings. Though you could cut the tension with a knife, Komachi's proposal turns the situation into a laid-back picnic chapter.

• The Tattooed Sisters
The two are bossed about, abandoned, and left perplexed by Alcina. They encounter the Furry-Ear Gang, Star Team, and Weekend's underlings, discover that they are Tower witches, and try to capture them as they should, but then Komachi turns the scene into a picnic as described above. The older sister of the two takes a spot next to Komachi to show her what a good girl she is.

Chapter 84

Alcina's witch trial.

• Takamiya
Forced to undergo Alcina's witch trial after being taken to the Chairwoman's room by Medusa. He is suspected of having ties to Kayou Kagari, leading Kagari and the other witches to do everything they can to clear his name.

• Atori
Under orders from Kagari, Atori has been keeping constant watch over Takamiya, to the point that she's made the attic in Takamiya's room her bed. She reports everything to Kagari, leaving Takamiya with just about zero secrets whatsoever.

• Kasumi

Comparatively, Kasumi doesn't keep many records at all. As she mostly takes baths with him, wears his clothes, and sleeps in the same bed as him, her diaries are filled with subjective impressions. They probably won't do much to address the false accusations being made in the trial.

• The Tattooed Sisters

These two videotape everything Takamiya does. On VHS. Following this trial, they and Atori held an information-trading session.

Chapter 85

Kayou appears.

• Takamiya

One of Kayou's underlings deceives Kiora and sneaks inside before using herself as a gate to successfully summon forth Kayou. Kayou then captures Takamiya.

Kayou, who has dedicated her life to the research of magic, has developed all sorts of magical goods not intended for mass-production, but in order to acquire a unique power.

Witchcraft Works

Flying Witch

Chihiro Ishizuka

Prepare to be Bewitched!

Makoto Kowata, a novice witch, packs up her belongings (including a black cat familiar) and moves in with her distant cousins in rural Aomori to complete her training and become a full-fledged witch.

"Flying Witch emphasizes that while actual magic is nice, there is ultimately magic in everything." — Anime News Network

The Basis for the Hit Anime from Sentai Filmworks!

Volumes 1-8 Available Now!

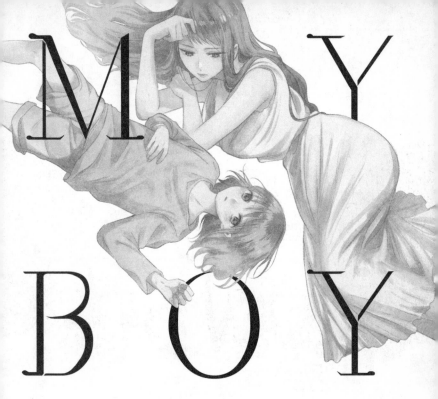

Hitomi Takano

Satoko Tawada, a 30-year-old office worker at a sporting goods company, encounters Mashuu Hayami, a 12-year-old boy, playing soccer in a park at night. She was treated cruelly by a former lover, he is dealing with a high-handed and uninvolved family. Both are burdened with loneliness, and they sense that the other has something that they're searching for...

"I was a little apprehensive about *My Boy*, but this opening volume is a fantastic entrance into the lives of Satoko and Mashuu: poignant, emotional, relatable. With plenty of story yet to reveal, I can see *My Boy* being 'all I end up thinking about'."   — *The OASG*

Volumes 1 - 6 Available Now!

THE GOLDEN SHEEP
KAORI OZAKI
"They say if you write down your wish, bury it under Sheep Tower and then dig it up after 7 years and 7 months, your wish will come true..."
Tsugu Miikura, a high schooler who loves to play guitar, had to move away from the rural town where she had spent her childhood due to family circumstances. After several years, she's back in her old hometown. She reunites with her childhood friends—Sora, Yuushin, and Asari—the friends she had buried a time capsule with back in elementary school. Tsugu is overjoyed to be with her friends once more, but the bonds that she thought would never change have in fact started to grow major cracks...
All 3 Volumes Available Now!

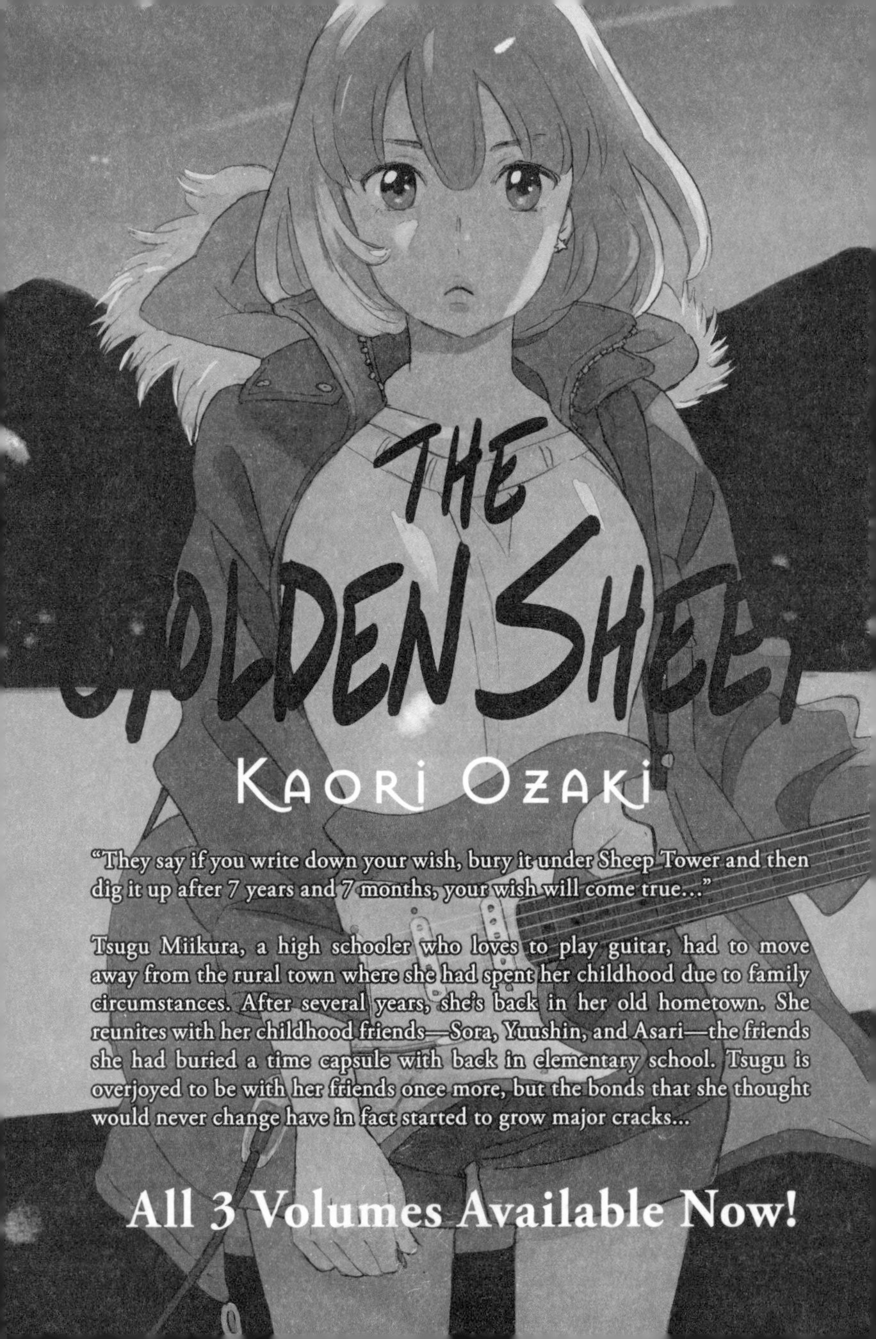

Witchcraft Works, volume 14

A Vertical Comics Edition

Translation: Ko Ransom
Production: Risa Cho
          Melissa DeJesus

Copyright © 2019 Ryu Mizunagi. All rights reserved.
First published in Japan in 2019 by Kodansha, Ltd., Tokyo
Publication rights for this English edition arranged through Kodansha, Ltd., Tokyo
English language version produced by Vertical Comics, an imprint of
Kodansha USA Publishing, LLC

Translation provided by Vertical Comics, 2020
Published by Kodansha USA Publishing, LLC, New York

Originally published in Japanese as *Uicchi Kurafuto Waakusu 14* by Kodansha, Ltd., 2019
Uicchi Kurafuto Waakusu first serialized in *good! Afternoon*, Kodansha, Ltd., 2010·

This is a work of fiction.

ISBN: 978-1-94998

Manufactured in (

First Edition

Kodansha USA Pu
451 Park Avenue
7th Floor
New York, NY 10016
www.readvertical.com

TEEN
WIT

Witchcraft Works:
Volume 14

12/01/20

MANGA